# Forever Across The Marsh

## A novel by Jeff Pearson

*I dedicate this book to my editor. She is smart, attractive, loving, strong, about five-foot-three, brown hair, hazel eyes, beautiful, and happens to be my wife.*

*I also dedicate this book to those who are struggling right now. I wrote this for you.*

## About the Author

Jeff Pearson grew up in Camden, South Carolina. At least, he tried to grow up. His brain got stuck somewhere between eight and eighteen years of age. After high school, he wanted to focus his efforts on hunting and fishing, but his parents convinced him to go to college. It was in college, at Clemson University, where Jeff really began to develop a talent for the absurd, likely because he was surrounded by some of the best in the business. This created an environment that encouraged somewhat of an arms race in humor.

Jeff then attended law school at George Washington University. After graduating, Jeff realized that he and his wife would be in debt for the rest of their lives. Then good fortune arrived—a prestigious law firm offered Jeff a job making more money than he had ever imagined. In a characteristic lapse of sanity, Jeff declined the offer and instead joined the United States Navy, thereby sealing his fate to remain forever in debt. The U.S. Navy sent Jeff to several exotic locations, including Afghanistan and Iraq, where Jeff had the luxury of serving in the Al Anbar province with the United States Marine Corps.

Soon after Jeff returned home from a trip to Afghanistan, the young couple's first child arrived. Then another. And another. And another. It was the experience of raising children that taught Jeff how precious and short life can be.

After leaving active duty, Jeff juggled two jobs— practicing law while also serving as a reservist in the Navy. He found both of these jobs difficult, but nowhere near as hard as trying to keep three small human beings alive while other things in life—primarily his house—tried to destroy him. Around him, Jeff saw others everywhere living in the same chaos, yet somehow making it through each day. At some point, Jeff said, "This is crazy!" Then he wrote *Forever Across The Marsh*.

# PART ONE

# CHAPTER 1

## *The Power of One*

S ome people are born for the cold. They can battle the wind and rain and snow all winter until the bitter end. They take pride in their ability to survive the harsh elements. They embrace winter and love winter to the point where their identity depends on winter. I am not one of these people.

My house sat in a small town near Savannah, Georgia. Savannah has two seasons—spring and summer. Sure, there are a few days of winter sprinkled about Christmas, but not enough to buy a jacket.

It was March. Pink and white azaleas lined the old roads and parks. The huge branches of ancient oaks stretched their arms toward one another, creating lazy tunnels of shade to cover those passing by. A park in March was the perfect place to get away from the daily struggles of the real world.

I closed my eyes and tried to feel the sunshine warm against my back. This was a challenge because I lived in Rhode Island. Still on active duty in the Navy, I had been stationed in Newport for two years.

March was no longer my friend. It was cold and rainy and cold. My two young children were still wrapped in their winter jackets and we were indoors. I had battled winter for months and winter had won. I formally surrendered by submitting my papers to be released from active duty. In typical bureaucratic form, the United States Navy did nothing. So I waited, still on duty.

My wife and I had recently bought a house near Savannah. It had been sitting empty for months, waiting for us to arrive. We needed to arrive. Paying a mortgage and rent is not easy when your bank account is dry. My string of bad decisions had rendered us poor. Not the kind of poor where you do not have any money. We were poorer than that. We had debt, mountains of it. Student loan debt, mortgage debt, old car debt, new car debt, credit card debt, personal loan debt, and it went on and on. As a service member, I made just enough to qualify for loans. I would have been better off without a job and flat broke.

On a frosty Sunday morning, I sat in a small chapel near the base with my wife and two children. As I looked out the window, my mind drifted off in a daydream. I knew the weather would turn, but not soon enough. I had long forgotten about the picture-perfect summers of Newport. The winter had blanketed over that distant glimmer of hope, as it did everything.

"You have a choice," the preacher said, interrupting my dream. "You can have a one-hundred-dollar bill right now or you can have this penny that doubles in value every day for thirty days. Which one would you choose?"

The sound of money made all my daydreams disappear. I looked about the room to find the congregation focused on the preacher.

"Which one would you take?" he repeated, holding up a fresh one-hundred-dollar bill next to a penny.

This was my kind of riddle. There was the certainty of math against the uncertainty of the mind.

"I know which one I would have chosen, if asked," he continued. "I would put that one-hundred-dollar bill in my pocket and go."

Many in the congregation smiled and nodded.

While others waited for the preacher's point, I wondered how much that magic penny was worth.

"Except I now know how much that penny is worth," he said. "A math teacher told me. Can you believe that penny will grow to over one billion pennies after only thirty days?"

Blasphemy! I thought. That is absolute mathematical blasphemy.

"That's right," he said. "This single penny would be worth over ten million dollars if it doubled in value every day for thirty days."

I looked around the room and saw that everyone again nodded and smiled. They all seemed to take the man at his word.

I doubted. Such a statement required proof. And proof I could provide without consulting another person or source. I could disprove or confirm his statement with the statement itself.

I began my calculations on the back of the church program.

Day 1: 2 cents.
Day 2: 4 cents.
Day 3: 8 cents.
Day 4: 16 cents.
Day 5: 32 cents.

Almost a week into it and I had not made fifty cents. Not enough to buy a good piece of candy.

Day 6: 64 cents.

Day 7: $1.28.

It took one week to break a dollar. It did not look good for the preacher's statement.

Day 8: $2.56.

Day 9: $5.12.

Day 10: $10.24.

After ten days, I had not made any real money, only a little more than ten dollars.

The preacher continued with his sermon. Everyone else still focused on his message. I found it hard to believe that I was the only one making calculations. Surely someone else shared my interest in the matter. I looked around and found that I was alone. Alone, but determined.

Day 11: $20.48.

Day 12: $40.96.

Day 13: $81.92.

Day 14: $163.84.

Ok. So it took almost half a month for the riddle to pay off. The one-hundred-dollar bill looked less appealing now. But we were still far from the promise of one billion pennies.

I heard the preacher's voice again and returned to my calculations.

Day 15: $327.68.

Day 16: $655.36.

Day 17: $1,310.72.

Day 18: $2,621.44.

Day 19: $5,242.88.

Day 20: $10,485.76.

I started to believe. Maybe he was right. I mean, in twenty days, that penny had grown to a small fortune, making that hundred-dollar bill a distant memory. I understood the power of exponential growth. But, still, only ten days remained.

I found comfort in the certainty and reliability of math. There were no holes in it.

The preacher continued and so did I.

Day 21: $20,971.52.

Day 22: $41,943.04.

Day 23: $83,886.08.

Day 24: $167,772.16.

Day 25: $335,544.32.

With five days remaining, I saw hope. We were within reach.

Day 26: $671,088.64.

Day 27: $1,342,177.28.

How that single penny had grown! In twenty-seven days, it had passed one million dollars. The outcome was all but certain now. The preacher was right. He had been right all along, probably without even knowing it.

In the face of this great discovery, my mind raced off to explore the possibilities. It was only a discovery to *me*. Of course, this penny always had the capacity to grow at such a rate. It had been that way from the beginning. But it meant so much more, now that I knew. What if I could double the value of a penny thirty times, not necessarily in thirty days, just thirty times? That feat would yield over ten million dollars, according to the preacher.

And what if we were not talking about pennies? This mathematical magic could apply to almost anything. A seed could double. A fire could double. Birth could double. Death could double. Cures could double. Disease could double. Bacteria, good and bad, could double. Almost anything could double.

Then I heard the preacher's voice again and my mind returned to the final calculations.

Day 28: $2,684,354.56.

Day 29: $5,368,709.12.

Day 30: $10,737,418.24.

There it was. In black and white with all its certainty. I sat there stunned as the preacher concluded his sermon, even though I did not hear another word.

This was the message I needed to hear, delivered when I needed to hear it. Despite having nothing, much less than nothing, I knew now that one day my family could be rich, or at least not broke. I now had hope.

CHAPTER 2

## *Night Diving*

Money meant nothing to Jesse.

He stood on the bow of his old sailboat, looking off into the night. To the east, bright stars sparkled against the dark sky. Behind him, to the west, stood Savannah's warm glow. Jesse peered once more toward the eastern horizon and sighed. Then he dove into the black salty water.

He could feel the water change from warm to cool and then from cool to cold as he swam deeper and deeper. At twenty feet, he felt the edge of the big hole. He swam deeper. At forty feet, he was more than halfway down the steep slope. At sixty feet, he neared the muddy bottom. This marked the edge of the deep hole. Most of the good stuff rested near the edge.

For over forty years, Jesse had conditioned his lungs by diving deeper and deeper for longer and longer. In the world of dark-water diving, he had no peers. Most could dive no more than fifteen feet.

He swam with his eyes closed. There was no use in keeping them open. At two feet, he could no longer see his own hand pressed against his nose.

Jesse navigated by other means, using a sixth sense of sort. He could sense the presence of a large shark, just as a shark could sense the presence of him. At times, Jesse sensed the presence of a large shark by detecting a subtle change in the current or a subtle noise or a vibration. Other times, Jesse sensed the presence of a shark by bumping against it. This bothered neither Jesse nor the shark. He would rather bump against a shark in those dark waters than bump against a stranger on a busy street. He put more trust in the shark. Aside from being hungry, a shark had no other reason to attack him. And the shark never took more than it needed. This, Jesse could respect.

Jesse had become one with the vast marsh. Life thrived in the marsh. Everything thrived. Fish, reptiles, birds, insects. Everything. All the animals knew Jesse as just another marsh creature. He was one of them. Even the bugs did not bother him.

The saltwater holes of Georgia were the deepest, darkest, and most treacherous of their kind. And these qualities gave Jesse sole custody of the treasure that rested in the mud.

Jesse felt along the bottom for the usual specimens. But this time he found something large. It was not a shark tooth. It was much bigger. Then he felt the familiar back row of flat teeth. It felt heavy stuck in the mud but light once he pulled it loose. He ascended to the surface with the find in his hand.

"Anything good?" Ruby asked.

Ruby spent many nights with Jesse on his boat. She enjoyed escaping to the quiet nights on the water. She often needed a recharge, especially after busy seasons in her line of work.

"A mastodon jaw," Jesse said.

"How much would it go for?"

"Probably around 10k if I sold it quick."

"A mastodon in Georgia. How grand!"

Jesse climbed aboard and put the jaw on the bow on top of dozens of large teeth and bones.

Since the beginning of time, the tide had swept back and forth over that deep hole, depositing anything that would sink. The same strong tides that had buried these treasures also kept humans away, the tides and the fear of sharks and alligators.

"Forty years of diving this hole and nothing has bit you. You ain't natural," Ruby said.

"Well, that makes two of us," Jesse said.

"Ten thousand dollars! I'm shopping for a dress with diamonds right now. Everyone will see Ms. Ruby when she walks downtown."

"That's right. And they'll wonder who you stole the money from."

"Let them wonder! I'll have my dress either way."

"Nobody's shopping for any dresses tonight. We're going to the shelf."

"There you go spoiling all my fun again. I guess you'll just have to hear me talk about my diamond dress until you see it on me."

Ruby sauntered down into the cabin. It was late and she wanted to sleep. She would never tell Jesse, but she loved the trips to the shelf on nights like this. The rhythm of the boat softly cutting through the waves lulled her to sleep. The cabin was small, but big enough. There was room for two to sleep, one on each side in coffin-like beds. She stretched her legs and laid down on a thin mattress. There was a glass-covered porthole next to her pillow. She looked out across the moonlit sound, looking forward to a deep, deep sleep.

Jesse pulled anchor and raised the jib. With the tide and a light breeze, he eased out of the river. At the mouth of the sound, the river's current and the outgoing tide met the incoming waves. Jesse raised the mainsail and headed out to the open sea. It was a good night with a full moon and a steady breeze. Over seventy miles beyond the islands sat the shelf. They would arrive around sunrise.

Jesse tied the lines and pointed the bow toward the east. Savannah's night glow slowly disappeared behind him. The old sailboat glided up and down the smooth waves; water lapping on the sides was the only sound.

Jesse piled his loot—three-weeks' worth—on the bow. There were three mastodon jaws. At least fifty megalodon teeth. Unidentified dinosaur bones. And the usual large shark teeth. He looked at the small fortune on his old boat and smiled. Then he went into the cabin and drifted off to sleep as his boat sailed away.

When the sun rose, so did Jesse, his boat gliding out to sea. He knew the rising sun would soon bring a change in the wind and churn the seas. He dropped the sails, bringing the boat to a rest. Stretching out his arms, he looked across the royal blue water. They were at the shelf. Hundreds of feet below, lay the ocean floor.

Far enough, he thought.

He gathered up all the bones and jaws and teeth and threw them overboard. Then he turned the boat to the west and sailed toward home.

## CHAPTER 3

# *On My Way Out*

I had heard the phrase "stop-loss" before, a few times from some senior officers who had served in Desert Storm, but most of us were not familiar with the concept. It did not happen often. I do not think it occurred at all during the eight years before I decided to leave active duty.

Everyone expected to deploy. Most wanted to deploy, that is, until they actually spent day after day for six to eighteen months in a hot, dusty wasteland. And then do it again. Misery cannot describe it.

But deployments were somewhat voluntary in the sense that one chose the line of work and expected to deploy. Just as I chose to join the service, I expected to leave the service when my obligation ended. It was a matter of choice. Stop-loss was different. And I did not recall ever seeing it in fine print or anywhere else. It was not the draft. Close. Maybe worse.

My executive officer, called XO by the unit, had called me into his office. I served in the Navy and he served in the Marine Corps, but we were a joint command, which meant he was my boss.

By custom and description, the XO enforces the rules. By personality and experience, my XO was a natural.

"Lieutenant Scott, you may be seated," he said.

"Thank you, sir."

Months earlier, I had submitted my request to be released from active duty. I only needed my detaching orders to make it official.

"So you want to quit, do you," he said.

"Sir?"

"I don't much like quitters."

I nodded.

"I understand you don't like it here in Rhode Island," he said.

"It's not that, sir. It's just time for me to move on."

"You can't take the winters, huh?"

"I can, sir. I just . . ."

"You know what I like about the winters?"

"No, sir."

"I like the cold."

I nodded.

"And I like the freezing rain."

I nodded.

"I like how the wind cuts at the flesh on my face."

I stared at him.

"Lieutenant Scott, do you know what I really like about our winter?"

"No, sir."

"It keeps the people away."

I nodded.

"Lieutenant Scott, you've been in the service how long? Eight years?"

"Yes, sir."

"Two deployments?"

"Yes, sir."

"Some tough duty."

"Wasn't too bad, sir."

"It was tough. I know. Deployed a few times myself," he said. "Three."

He just looked at me.

"I thought about getting out once," he said.

"Really?"

"That's right, in the nineties. Then I got stop-lossed."

Silence.

"Stop-lossed?" I asked.

"That's right, stop-lossed. I actually put my papers in, just like you," he said, grinning at me. "Then Desert Storm happened and the Marine Corps decided that it was better for me and better for the Corps to keep me in the service. Sent me immediately to the sandbox."

I nodded.

"Best-damned thing that ever happened to me."

I nodded.

"You know it's hot right now in Afghanistan. A lot of action. Real hot."

"Yes, sir."

"A lot going on. They need good men over there."

Silence.

"They could even use you."

Silence.

"That's a joke, Lieutenant Scott. You're supposed to laugh. You're laughing, right."

"Yes, sir."

"Good."

"Sir?"

"Yes."

"Which part was the joke? The part about them needing me or the part about me being a . . ."

"Look, don't interrupt me. I don't have much time and this is important."

"Understood, sir."

"I'm trying to help you. Even though you're in the Navy, I like you. You're almost a Marine, but you're not. You're still a squid. Now, you want to quit the service and move to Virginia, right?"

"Savannah, sir."

"Savannah?"

"Yes, sir."

Silence.

"Hell. You said Savannah? That's right next to Parris Island!"

"Yes, sir."

"You're moving there?"

"Yes, sir."

"And I assume that's what you want to do more than anything else right now."

He paused, thought for a moment, and then continued.

"Look, Lieutenant Scott. What I'm about to tell you isn't going to be easy."

This is not good, I thought.

"This is a very tough conversation to have."

I better not be stop-lossed, I thought.

"You've deployed. Twice."

Yes. Eighteen-months apiece.

"Taken tough duty."

Yeah, I'd say three years away from my family was tough, I thought.

"I've done tough duty. Three deployments."

You said that already.

"You have children."

Yes. They recently accepted me as a real person, not just a picture and a voice on the phone.

"And you want to leave the service."

"Yes, sir."

"You prepared for this."

Well, I thought, I used all of my savings for a down payment on a house I've never seen in a town I've never been to. I am now in debt up to my neck. I bought a van. Another seven years of debt. Two children. No job yet. But all of that is better than the possibility of leaving my family again to spend eighteen months in a desert.

"Yes, sir," I said.

"Parris Island was tough. Deployments were tough."

Sure, whatever, just tell me where I'm deploying and let us get this over with. Then he started to look away, off into the distance, the thousand-mile stare I had seen many times before.

"I remember my tours. It was hot. It was so hot over there. We couldn't go outside. It was just too hot."

He started shaking. The flashback had taken over.

"Then it cools down. That's when they start moving. They start looking for you. It's like they only try to kill you when the weather was good."

I started to worry. I too remembered those days and I did not find it helpful to dwell on them. I remembered how insurgents would ambush convoys during good weather. That was when they laid the most IEDs. They were lazy insurgents, but deadly when it was convenient. XO must have witnessed the same. Nothing over there seemed to change.

"Without warning, they would surround you," he said. "That's when all hell broke loose."

He started to twitch. His eyes welled up. I knew I had to say something. Anything. It was just too pitiful to see XO cry.

"Sir, I know what you're talking about. I've been there."

"You've been there!" he yelled. "You've been there! You're sitting there in your white Navy uniform telling me you've been there!"

He now stared wild daggers at me.

"And now," he said. "You're going back."

I could not believe it. My worst fear had come true.

"Understood, sir."

"No, I don't think you do."

"But, sir . . ."

"This is no time to 'but, sir' me. Look, I'm trying to help you out. All you can say is 'understood, sir'."

"Sir, with all due respect, I have deployed twice."

"Deployment! Who the hell is talking about deployment! I'm talking about Savannah! You're about to leave the best-damned thing that happened to you and move to an uninhabitable swamp! Deployment would be a vacation compared to living in that bug-infested mud hole!"

"Say that again, sir?"

"A swamp! Squid. Savannah is uninhabitable!"

Then something really set him off.

"You can't go outside! Ever! In the summer, it's too damned hot. Then when it cools, the bugs come out! It's absolutely uninhabitable!"

"Bugs. You mean, roaches?"

"Roaches! You ask me about roaches!"

He paused, and then started to smile.

"Wait a second, Lieutenant Scott. Have you ever lived in Savannah?"

"No, sir."

He started to laugh.

"And you ask if they have roaches."

He rose from his chair and began pacing back and forth.

"When I see a dark spot on the floor at night," he said, "I step on it."

"Yes, sir, so do I."

"Right after I scream like a little girl."

"That's a little different, sir."

"Then I step on it again and again, just to make sure it's dead."

"Ok, sir."

"Then I see that the spot is just a bleeping leaf," he said, using the Marine Corps version of bleeping. "Lieutenant Scott, we don't have roaches here in Rhode Island. The cold doesn't allow it."

"Yes, sir."

"You know what I do next?"

"No, sir."

"I step on it again. And again. And again. I continue to step on it until I'm sure I've killed that bleeping leaf! Do you understand!"

"No, sir."

"Exactly. That's the point."

Silence.

"And you're worried about roaches," he said.

A serious but mad look formed on his hardened face.

"They have seasons for each bug," he said.

Complete silence.

"There's a mosquito season," he said.

"And a horsefly season."

"And a black fly season."

"All of these creatures have one purpose in life—to chew on your flesh."

Silence.

"And none of these are half as bad as the worst."

Silence.

"Have you ever been attacked by a swarm of invisible, man-eating insects?"

"No, sir."

"Have you ever walked outside to get the morning paper and before you can take five steps, thousands of flesh-eating bugs attack every inch of your exposed skin?"

"No, sir."

"Lieutenant Scott, do know what my hardest duty was— of all the duty I've ever had?"

"No, sir."

"Standing at attention at Parris Island."

His whole body began to twitch.

"I'd rather be in the desert with people shooting at me. I'd rather suffer for twelve months from an internal bacterial infection. Diarrhea every day. Then burn it and have to smell shit in the air every day for twelve months. That's nothing compared to one day at Parris Island when the bugs are out."

Silence.

"Lieutenant Scott. Congratulations. You have just won the national championship of making stupid decisions."

He sat down and at least pretended to regain his composure.

"Lieutenant Scott, what is your plan?"

"Plan, sir?"

"Yes, a plan. You do have a plan, right? How are you going to make a living and feed your family? That sort of plan."

"Well, I have to, sir."

"You have to what?"

"I have to, sir. I have no savings."

Silence.

"Because I bought a house."

Silence.

"And a van."

Silence.

"I'm in debt for the next thirty-seven years."

"I see," he said.

"I also have two young children."

"Humph."

"So, I have no choice but to make it happen."

Silence.

He looked at the ceiling then back at me. He scratched his head as if he were thinking about what exactly to say.

"So, you're telling me that you're surrounded?"

"Yes, sir."

"Completely surrounded?"

"Yes, sir."

He paused.

"Good. I like it. You can shoot in any direction."

He reached down and found a folder with my name on it.

"Here are your detaching orders. You can depart today."

"Thank you, sir," I said. "Permission to leave, sir?"

"Permission granted."

I stood up.

"And Lieutenant Scott," he said, "watch out for those bugs."

"Yes, sir."

Before I left the room, I looked back.

"Sir?"

"Yes, Lieutenant Scott."

"At least they'll keep the people away."

He looked at me and smiled, a very mad smile.

## CHAPTER 4

# *Jesse's Island*

As evening approached, Jesse sailed past the barrier islands and returned to the sound. The setting sun turned the sky a purple orange and the water gold.

Jesse had seen this bit of magic more than a thousand times. "Damn, that's beautiful," he said aloud to himself.

As far as he could see, there were no other boats, just his little sailboat gliding back to the island. He wondered how it had stayed this way for so long. The stretch of marsh was one of the few places not yet touched by mankind.

Someday, they will come, he thought. And fill this place with bridges and resorts and stores and factories and everything else that follows in the wake of progress.

He pointed the bow of his boat toward his island and caught a steady breeze. Then, without warning, he sensed something out of order. He was certain something was different. A few minutes later, he saw it—a small, dark boat, less than three miles away.

I do not like it, he thought. He knew all the boats in this area, but not that one. And he had seen it before, in the same place.

Maybe I should stay on a different island, he thought. Or anchor out here for the night. Or I could sail all the way back to Savannah and drop Ruby off, he thought.

"Ruby, are you awake?" Jesse asked.

"No!"

"I was thinking about taking you into town."

"What? I thought we were going back tomorrow."

Jesse reconsidered. Changing my course will not do any good, he thought. If they're watching me, then they'll be back again. And if I go somewhere else, they'll know I'm watching them.

"Never mind," he said. "We'll stay on the island tonight."

Jesse's island was like many of the smaller islands scattered about the vast marsh. A mixture of tall pines, live oaks, and palmettos lined the edges of its bluffs. The island was like a small plateau sitting about ten feet above the marsh. There were hundreds of these islands and they were all flat, just like the marsh. Jesse wondered if a glacier had been there millions of years ago, cutting out the land as it passed.

The landward islands did not change in shape or size, unlike the larger barrier islands, which changed in shape and size every year from the storms as they protected all the other islands from the sea. Then there were the underwater islands, appearing above the surface only at certain tides. Like the barrier islands, these changed over time. Maps could not keep up with these islands, so only the regular watermen could navigate the waters with confidence.

This had always been the way of the marsh, which is one reason why it served as a haven for pirates during their reign. Both legend and truth told stories of pirates running shallow draft boats over the bars at just the right tide, luring enemies to do the same. Except the enemy would run aground.

The marsh had once been thick with pirates and Savannah's port had served them well, resting between the more established settlements in South Carolina and Florida. Georgia had been a buffer state between the two, and in some ways, still is.

Jesse's island enjoyed one way in and one way out by water. Time and nature had cut a slough that zigzagged to the center of the island, where it emptied into a deep hole. At low tide, the slough dried up, most of it anyway. Between the main waterway and the deep hole sat a never-ending layer of mud. Thick suck mud.

Jesse dropped his sails and floated into the island with the tide. Along the banks were herons, otters, deer, alligators, and a host of other native animals that generally ignored Jesse's presence. No birds flew away. The alligators did not alter their course. The otters and deer continued to rummage for food without even looking up. Jesse was as much a part of the island as any other animal, perhaps more so. He had lived there longer than any other creature. So, to the native inhabitants, it would be odd if Jesse were not there. They knew no other way.

Jesse caught fish and shrimp from his tidal creek, but harmed no animal unless he needed it for food.

Several of the alligators stretched over fifteen feet and eight hundred pounds. At times, Jesse would swim at night with these same beasts at his side, neither Jesse nor the alligators thinking much of it.

His boat glided to a stop at the edge of the deep hole. Jesse tied the boat to a large oak bending over the water and then walked toward home. Feeling the boat stop, Ruby followed.

Around him, Jesse heard birds singing in the trees. He heard deer walking in the water. He heard his footsteps along with Ruby's. But he heard no sounds from city streets. No hum of engines. No machinery. No trains. Nothing to intrude upon the natural harmony on the island.

Long ago, Jesse had built his own house.

It was a tall white house, much like a lighthouse, but there was only one floor. He had built steps spiraling up the wall so he could climb to the top. At the top, were four large openings, positioned at north, east, south, and west. From these openings, he could look across the marsh and to the ocean as far as one could see. During hot days, the openings allowed wind to blow across the top of his dwelling, pulling out hot air. All the walls, inside and out, were painted white. The roof was painted white. This kept the heat at bay and the ground floor always remained cool.

Inside were two hammocks, a table, and two chairs. Nothing else. Because he needed nothing else.

Jesse had built an outside cooking area with a large outdoor fireplace and a table. He had installed a faucet and pipes to pull running water from a nearby spring.

Jesse and Ruby sat down at the table.

"Most people think I'm a witch," Ruby said.

Jesse nodded.

"And," she said, "I think you're strange."

"Thank you."

"You are a strange, strange man."

Jesse smiled and then poured a cup of cool water for himself and for Ruby.

"You risk your skin for those bones just to throw them away. Why don't you buy something nice for once, like a diamond dress for your girlfriend?"

"You have money."

"Yes, but I don't have no dress from my boyfriend."

"What is a witch going to do with a diamond dress?"

"Make them look at me, that's what. I'll walk down River Street and make them look at me. Up and down that street. I'll just walk. And they'll just talk."

"You're crazy."

"So tell me, island man, why was it you wanted to go to Savannah tonight?"

"I saw a boat."

"What do you mean 'I saw a boat'? I need you to tell me what you're feeling, man. I don't need to know nothing about no boat."

"I saw a boat. About three miles away. Never seen it before. It is very odd for it to be out here at all, much less in the middle of the week."

"Don't give me any of your silly logic. Mr. 'I saw a boat.' It's just a boat. But I know that you know more. You could sense it. I know you could feel it in your bones. There's something dark in that boat. And don't tell me otherwise. That is my business and I know my business."

Ruby was right. Jesse knew she was right. The crazy old devil woman had been reading people her entire life. It was her business and her gift. Ruby was a witch if there ever were one. Her clients knew this. That was why some traveled for thousands of miles for her services.

"We'll see," Jesse said. "But we're staying here tonight. Tomorrow, we'll go out with the tide, just like we always do."

CHAPTER 5

# On the Road

I left my XO's office convinced he had lost his mind. My sister and her husband had lived in Savannah and they never complained about the heat or the bugs or anything else. They were always talking about how wonderful it was in Savannah and that we should move near them and raise our children near their children. It all sounded right and perfect to us, even though they did not have any children and had not lived in Savannah for very long.

Rushing back to our small, old apartment, I could think of nothing except having my detaching orders in hand.

I wanted to get on the road as soon as possible and I knew that Lynn would share my enthusiasm. At the same time, I did not want the joy to overwhelm her like it did me. Maybe I should tell her about it calmly and slowly, I thought. Yes, that would be the right approach—let it sink in first. The wonderful shock might be too much. I decided to tell her while holding a straight poker face as long as possible.

We were ready. All we had to do was get in the van and go. That would take less than two hours. I ran into the kitchen waving the orders above my head and yelled, "I have my orders! Let's go to Savannah!"

Lynn was packing some of the last boxes and cleaning up a mess the kids had just made.

"That's nice, dear," she said.

"We're going to Savannah!"

"Can you push the couch away from the wall? I need to vacuum around the baseboards," she said.

"Baseboards? Look! Look at this. I have my orders!"

"If you get that side, I can get this side. That way we don't scratch the floors."

"Ok, I'm picking it up. Where do you want me to . . . wait a second," I said, dropping the couch. "Did you hear what I just said? We can leave! To Savannah!"

"Yes, I heard you but we have so many things to do before we go."

"Things? To do?"

"Yes."

"Things, like baseboards?"

"Yes. And we need to mop the floors and dust the windows. There are some spots where Tyler and Sophia spilled juice on the carpet. The kitchen is a mess."

"Doesn't our lease require us to pay a cleaning fee?"

"Yes."

"So, someone else will clean it when we leave."

"Yes."

"Someone other than you and me."

"Yes."

We just stared at each other.

"So . . . why don't we let someone else clean it?" I asked.

"That's just ridiculous. We can't leave the apartment like it is. We have to clean it."

"I don't understand."

"Of course you don't. Now just move that couch and let's get to work."

"But . . ." I began, but better judgment silenced me.

Three days later, we had almost finished Lynn's checklist. We piled our stuff and our kids into our new van and left the little apartment behind us.

"So, we're really doing it," I said.

"Doing what?" she asked.

"You know, moving on. Starting a new chapter. Making it on our own."

"Yes, there is a lot we need to do, especially to the house."

"I can't believe I have not seen the house yet. It'll be good to do some of the repairs myself. Did you know that I always wanted to build my own house? It's a good thing we didn't hire someone else to do everything before we moved in."

"I guess," she said.

"We really are doing it," I said, as the highway raced behind us.

Lynn looked out the window.

"We bought a house," I said.

All was quiet, even the kids did not make a sound.

"We bought a van," I continued.

She nodded.

"There's no turning back now. We've really burned our boats."

"What did you say?" she asked. "You bought a boat?"

"Hooray!" Tyler shouted.

"No. No. No. I didn't buy a boat. I said we burned our boats."

Blank stares from both.

"You know, like Hernando Cortes did."

"Well, I don't know anything about this Cortes friend of yours and I really don't care why he burned his boat. I just know we're not getting a boat."

"No. Cortes. The Spanish conquistador. You know, he landed on the shores of Mexico and told his troops that there's no going back and ordered them to set fire . . ."

"Dad?" Tyler asked. "Why did your friend burn his boat?"

"Look. Nobody burned his boat."

"But you just said . . ."

"It's just a saying. What I meant was that we have destroyed all possible ways of going back to our prior way of life and have no choice but to succeed in our next adventure."

"Ok," he said.

"And that there's nothing but blue skies and good fortune ahead for us."

"Dad?"

"Yes, Son?"

"Can we get a boat?"

"Yes. Of course."

"No," Lynn said. "We're not getting a boat."

"Well, not right away, but maybe in a few months, if we see a good deal . . ."

"No. We're not getting a boat. They're nothing but trouble. We might as well burn our money."

"Mommy?"

"Yes, dear."

"Why did we burn our money?"

"We didn't. Well, unless you consider . . . never mind. Buying a boat would be like burning our money. I really don't understand why people want to own a boat anyway."

"What do you mean?" I said. "Boats are great. It's a fantastic way for the family to spend time together."

"We can spend time together on dry land, in the backyard, without wasting money we don't have. And besides, you would only use a boat once or twice a year. If you really want to float around in a boat for whatever reason, we can rent one."

"Don't be silly," I said. "No one rents a boat. That's like renting a dog or something."

"Daddy?" Tyler said. "Are we getting a dog?"

"No," Lynn said. "We're not getting a dog or renting a dog or borrowing a dog or . . ."

"Look, honey," I said. "Maybe you just need to spend a little more time with boats so you can understand them. Maybe have some empathy for boats, put yourself in their shoes and see how it feels."

"What are you talking about? The answer is no. I understand boats. They are a waste of money and dangerous. Every time you go out on a boat, you come home smelling of booze and bragging about how everyone on the boat nearly died. How is that fun or safe or, under any rational reasoning, a good way for our family to spend time together?"

"Just hear me out for a minute. Imagine yourself on the bow of a boat, the wind gently blowing your hair back. You are sipping a piña colada, floating toward a beach off the coast of Savannah."

"Did the engine break down?" she asked.

"No. The engine didn't break down."

"You said we were floating toward some island. And I know boats well enough to know that the engines are always breaking down."

"That's ridiculous. People just think the engine is going to break down. It never actually breaks down," I said.

"What about that time when you and your dad . . ."

"Let's stay focused here. You're on a boat. You have a piña colada. I'm driving. The wind is softly blowing across my face, I mean, your face. I have one hand on the steering wheel and one on a nice cold, uh . . . , piña colada that I'm giving to you."

"You said I already had one."

"Dad?" Tyler asked.

"Yes, Son."

"Is the boat about to break down now?"

"No. Please stop," I said. "Both of you. And let me finish. What I'm trying to say is . . ."

"Mel! Watch out!" Lynn screamed.

All I saw were red brake lights. I swerved and somehow missed the car in front of us. But this put us in a violent spin at about seventy miles per hour down the interstate.

Lynn screamed. Tyler screamed. Sophia screamed.

A plastic bottle rolled under the accelerator and jammed.

We spun over a hill and I saw the disaster approaching fast. A line of cars and a crowd of people stood in the road. We were racing out of control toward the crowd and cars.

I looked at Lynn and saw the horror on her face. She was still screaming. So were Tyler and Sophia. Acting out of pure instinct, I kicked the plastic bottle with all my might.

Now the pedal was stuck. For good. We raced faster and faster.

I pumped the brakes hard but this only launched us into a more violent spin.

I have heard others speak of how time slows down as death approaches. For me, time disappeared completely. I looked at Lynn and saw her close her eyes. I looked at Tyler and Sophia. They were scared and confused. I looked one more time at my wife. It was unavoidable and I knew it. I let go of the wheel and I too closed my eyes.

I cannot explain with words what happened next, only that overwhelming peace came over me. It was the single most peaceful moment in my life. I floated away to where I hovered above my family below, all together in that spinning van. Then I heard a voice, that of a young girl. A voice, it seemed, I had heard over a thousand times. But a voice, I also knew, I was hearing for the first time.

"It's going to be all right," she said. "It's not your time."

CHAPTER 6

## *Ruby*

Pastor David loved routines. At exactly 6:30 AM every morning, Pastor David ate oatmeal, plain oatmeal without any sugar or butter or anything else that might harm his body. At 7:00 AM, he read the daily news. At 7:15 AM, he worked on his weekly sermon, but he stopped at 8:00 AM. There were other routines that needed tending to.

His grass always looked perfect. His house always stayed clean. Each tool in his garage had a place and remained in its place unless being used.

Every day looked almost the same as the day before, except for the Sabbaths. He observed two Sabbaths, one on Saturday and the other on Sunday. He dedicated Saturday to the traditions of the Old Testament and Sunday to the New Testament.

Pastor David loved traditions, especially ancient ones. Easter would arrive in three days and there was much to do.

"Can we take the day off?" his wife asked.

"What do you mean 'take the day off?'" he asked.

"I don't know, maybe drive into Savannah. It is so beautiful in the spring. I'm sure there is a lively festival on River Street."

"But what about all our preparations?"

"Maybe we could skip a few this year. We could just go for a couple of hours and come back quickly."

"The corned beef alone will take all day to cook. The recipe calls for at least one hour of preparation. And I'll need to check it and baste it every forty-five minutes."

"Perhaps we could just put it in the slow cooker?"

"But the recipe calls for soaking it first and then baking it and then covering it with foil."

Pastor David loved recipes. Recipes had never failed him. He was known for preparing perfect meals, the kind that looked exactly like the picture in the recipe book. Pastor David was a reserved, quiet man, but a confident one. He had earned his confidence through repeated success in everything he did.

He knew that life was easy if you just followed instructions. The instructions were there for a reason. They were there because they worked. In a recipe, any deviation from the instructions would result in something different from what you wanted to achieve. To prepare a proper meal, one simply needed to have patience and follow the recipe, all the steps, including the preparation steps.

"We'll need eight ounces of chopped onions," he said.

"Two tablespoons of garlic," he said.

"One tablespoon of coriander," he said.

"I really want to go to Savannah," she said. "Please."

Pastor David loved routines, but he loved his wife even more.

"Ok, dear. We'll go, but only for two or three hours to-tal. That's how much time I allocated for the corned beef. We can make the corned beef another day. I will find a place for it on our calendar of meals."

"Thank you. Are you sure you don't want to put it in the slow cooker?"

"Yes, dear, I'm sure. Let's go."

Pastor David knew that a recipe not followed was best not followed at all.

Pastor David drove down the long road to the interstate. For miles, he saw nothing but pine forests, something he knew would change soon, probably in his lifetime. People were moving to town. Fast. He thought, maybe that was why I felt called to move here years ago. When he had first moved to the town, there was nothing, just one traffic light in the main intersection. Now, the signs of growth were unmistakable.

On the way into town, he saw his small church.

"We need to plan for rapid growth," he said.

His wife nodded her head.

"This must have been why we were called to come here," he said.

She nodded again.

"It is all making perfect sense now. With the growth, there will be great opportunity to change lives," he said.

And for the rest of the drive, he planned and organized the steps his church needed to take to welcome new residents. They would need a larger worship center. An activity center. A larger parking lot. There was plenty of room for this growth because he had planned for the growth long ago, long before any signs of growth. I have built this church on solid rock, he thought, just as one's faith should be built. Now he had reason to build it larger and stronger.

Savannah had grown up long ago. The streets were alive with people, especially during spring, the high season for festivals and anyone selling anything. Everyone prospered during spring. They had to, for the spring carried them through the year. Artists depended on the season for their year's income. Streetside stores and restaurants relied on the festivals to survive. A bar closed on St. Patrick's Day would not make it to Labor Day.

This spring was no exception. River Street, an old cobblestone road along the river, was full to the brim with craftsmen and artists selling their wares. Crowds flowed up and down the cobblestone road looking for something special to buy.

It had been this way forever. The main part of Savannah sat high above River Street on a large bluff along the Savannah River. This arrangement provided the stores with perfect natural protection from floods and storms. The river always remained deep enough for large ships to safely navigate in and out of the city. All of this invited commerce. Savannah sat high on the bluff in stark contrast to the vast, flat marsh that flanked the rest of the Savannah River.

"It sure is nice to get out of town sometimes," his wife said. "Oh, look at these wonderful paintings."

"Yes, it is a gift to paint that way," he said.

"And those birds! Look at those wooden birds. I need to touch one to make sure it can't fly away."

"Amazing," he said, as they strolled from booth to booth.

"Oh my!" she said, pointing to another booth.

"What is it?"

Ruby's earrings fell below her shoulders. Her nails of different colors and sizes rested on a table. Her deep red dress stood out among the rainbow of pastels that others wore, but it was her eyes that got one's attention. They were bright and wild like her smile.

Jesse sat beside her in a booth selling his shark teeth.

"What is she selling?" Pastor David's wife asked.

"Don't know. I can't read her sign. Let's get closer."

"What does her sign say?"

"It says, let's see," Pastor David said. "I think it says, 'Devil's Friend.'"

"Oh my."

Pastor David and his wife walked over to Ruby's booth.

"Good afternoon, sir, madam," Ruby said. "What can I do for you?"

"We are curious. What is your business, ma'am?" Pastor David asked.

"My business, you ask. That depends on what you need," she said.

"I beg your pardon?"

"I provide certain services," she said. "Some call me a fortune teller, a seer, a mystic."

"Most call her a witch," Jesse said.

"Oh dear," Pastor David's wife said.

"Mind him none," Ruby said. "He's just a crazy old man who sells teeth."

"Well," Pastor David said, "it was nice to meet you both, but we are just looking and not interested in teeth or fortune telling today."

"I'm sorry to hear that," Ruby said. "I was going to offer you a free reading, sir."

Pastor David paused. Then his wife whispered to him, "I think we should go. I don't like this one bit."

"I agree," Pastor David whispered. "But it is free with no obligation. Maybe I can help this woman in some way."

"No, dear. Let's go."

"Ma'am," Pastor David said to Ruby. "Thank you very much. But we must go."

Ruby looked at him and caught his eyes. Pastor David could not look away. She stared at him for a moment, and then said, "Rabbi, I ask that you stay."

The shock of it took Pastor David back. He had not been called that in years and certainly not by this woman or anyone else in Georgia.

"Why did you call me that?" he asked, taking a seat across from Ruby. "How did you know I had once been a rabbi?"

Ruby laughed.

"Sir, my services are still free. May I please hold your hands?"

Pastor David extended his hands. Ruby held them and closed her eyes. Ruby began to breathe deep and slow until she slipped into a meditative state. Although Ruby's rhythm was slow and steady, her spell worked fast and Pastor David's head dropped.

"I am fortunate today," Ruby said. "I sense many connections. Many, many connections."

Pastor David began to speak, but thought otherwise.

"You have touched the lives of many. It has not been forgotten. Not among the ones who are still among us."

Pastor David relaxed a little more.

"The living might forget, but not the others."

The rhythm of Ruby's breathing thickened his tongue. Soon, he could not speak if he wanted to.

"Your work. It's difficult. Very difficult."

His eyes felt heavy. Soon he was out, but could hear Ruby's voice loud and clear.

"Pastor," she said.

He remained asleep, except to her.

"Pastor," she said.

"Yes," he replied, though he slept.

"Do you want to speak to any of those you have touched?"

"To who?"

"Any of them. Any who have gone before you."

"Who?"

"The dead."

"No. They are gone."

"No. They are not."

"I don't understand."

"You do."

"But they are gone."

"Pastor, let go."

She paused.

"Let go," Ruby continued.

He did not respond.

"Pastor, I sense your struggle."

"Yes."

"I can help. Speak to them."

He felt something approaching. The hairs on his neck rose. He felt it calling him, but he resisted.

"Speak to them. Ask them."

It felt closer.

"Wake up! Wake up!"

He opened his eyes.

"Honey, wake up!"

He looked around. Ruby was back too.

"Honey, you scared me. Please, let's go," Pastor David's wife said as she pulled at his arm.

"I'm sorry, dear, was it something I said?" Pastor David asked.

"Something you said? You didn't say a thing. You were hunched over mumbling incoherently back and forth with this woman. I thought you had a stroke or something."

"No, dear. I'm fine."

Ruby sat there, neither smiling nor frowning.

"And Ms. . . . , what is your name?" Pastor David's wife asked Ruby.

"They call her Ruby," Jesse said.

"Well, Ms. Ruby, what exactly were you doing to my husband?"

"I have no secrets, madam," Ruby said. "I was simply talking to him."

"It's true, honey, she was just talking to me."

"I do not believe it. She had you under some kind of trance."

"Madam," Ruby said, "we were talking. And you interrupted us."

"I think we're done here. Let's go," Pastor David's wife said.

"But Pastor," Ruby said, "what about your fortune?"

"Just a moment, dear," Pastor David said to his wife. "Please."

"What exactly were you doing?" he asked.

"I simply offered to put you in touch with the dead."

"Oh dear! This is too much," his wife said.

"I take it you don't believe in ghosts, madam."

"Ghosts? Of course not," Pastor David's wife replied.

"You know, Savannah is full of ghosts," Ruby said.

"Full of ghost stories, that is all. Nothing but a trap for tourists."

"They were here long before tourists."

"We don't believe in ghosts."

Ruby looked at Pastor David and asked, "You believe, don't you, sir?"

"Well, it is difficult for someone in my profession to believe in ghosts," Pastor David replied.

"What about angels?" Ruby asked.

"Well, that is different," he said.

"And what about the one you call the Holy Ghost?"

"Well, that is different, too," he said.

"Tell me, Pastor, who are you talking to when you pray?"

"I think I see your point. But you must understand that I see things differently than maybe you do."

"Maybe," she said. "Do you want your fortune? It is free and will only take a minute."

"Can I keep my eyes open?" he asked.

"Yes. Of course. Please hold out your hand."

"No hands this time, please," he said.

"No hands. Just open your hand. I have something to give you."

Pastor David opened his hand and Ruby gave him a red stone.

"What is this?" he asked.

"It is a Devil's Stone and it's yours to keep. And it is quite expensive, I must add," she said.

"But I really did not come here to buy anything."

"It is yours. No charge."

"Ok. Thank you. But please understand that I would rather not keep something called Devil's Stone," Pastor David said.

"You can give it back," Ruby said.

"Thank you."

"But not until after three days."

"Three days?"

"In three days, you will lose your faith, Rabbi."

"I think you are mistaken."

"We will see. In three days."

"You can have your stone now," Pastor David said.

"Please, Pastor. Keep it for three days. If I am wrong, bring it back to me. And I will repent and I will pray with you."

She had put him in a corner now. It was his duty as a pastor to pray for those who needed it. And this woman offered just that. It would be an easy task, he thought. Just wait three days. Then bring the stone back.

Pastor David rose from his seat.

"Easter is three days away. I will see you on Monday," he said.

"I will be here," she said.

"Will 9:00 AM work?"

"Yes."

"Then I will see you at 9:00 AM on Monday. Good day to you both," he said.

He put the stone in his pocket and left.

CHAPTER 7

# *Brain Power*

I always suspected that my brain was amazing. Our drive to Savannah proved this suspicion true. I have a theory that most people forget things, both little things and big things, and their forgetfulness is due in large part to a coping mechanism that has evolved over time, a coping mechanism that has helped the human race to survive and procreate. My brain, however, has an unparalleled capacity to forget almost anything, almost immediately and I am thankful for it.

Our van came to a stop and I returned from my brief dream.

"I can't believe we didn't crash," Lynn said.

"Me too," I said.

"I mean, I was certain we were going to hit that line of cars. I didn't think there was any way around it."

"Me too."

"I'm so glad you were driving. There's no way I could have handled it so well. I had no idea you had that ability. Really, I don't know how you did it. It was too much for me. I closed my eyes."

"Me too."

"What! You closed your eyes!"

"Well, I mean, we were going so fast and there were cars everywhere and I saw you close your eyes."

"I wasn't driving!"

"Yes, but I thought you had given up and it seemed reasonable at the time to give up."

"I was praying!"

"Oh."

"I can't believe you closed your eyes."

"Uh . . ."

"You were driving! With our entire family in it! You could have killed everyone, including our two young children and our unborn child."

"I know, but, hey, wait a second. Did you say unborn child?"

"Yes," Lynn said.

"So . . ."

"Yes."

"You mean . . ."

"Yes."

"How do you know?"

"I just do. It's a woman thing. Sometimes we just know."

"Well, maybe we should do a test," I said.

"Yes, we'll do a test soon."

"What are you talking about, Daddy?" Tyler asked.

"Nothing, Son. Just a mommy and daddy thing," I said.

"There's a gas station at the next exit," I told Lynn. "Maybe they have a test."

"We're not doing a pregnancy test at a gas station."

"Why not?"

"Just drive, please."

Lynn looked out the window, holding her stomach.

"Dad?"

"Yes, Son?"

"Why is Mommy mad at you?"

"She's not mad at me, she's just . . ."

I looked at Lynn. I had known her for many years and it was clear that she was mad at me.

"Honey," I said. "Did I say something?"

"No. Just drive, please."

"Honey?" I said, trying to come up with just the right thing to say.

"Just drive."

"I love you."

She did not say anything and she did not need to. I had no idea at the time she had such strong feelings about gas stations. Considering the circumstances, I thought it to be in everyone's best interest for me to just shut up.

Another child, I thought. Wow! Another child. I thought two was it. Sure, there was always the possibility of a third, but it wasn't the sort of thing rational, broke parents did on purpose. Another child. I would need to find a job and health insurance soon. Another child. Wow. Another child. It could be a boy or a girl. Who knows! Another child.

After the shock and exhaustion faded, I began to feel the thrill of another child. I loved my two children. And we were going to have another one! This meant we would need to get prepared—three baseball gloves, three fishing poles, three of everything. All right! Another child!

The news had erased the recent near-death experience from my brain, one of nature's coping mechanisms at work. Now, all I could think about was our new baby on the way. Nothing could tear my focus away from that.

"Hey, Dad," Tyler said. "Is that the kind of boat we are going to buy?"

The beauty of it all pushed me back in the seat and I almost let go of the steering wheel. Ahead of us, a sleek, white center console with three outboard engines on its transom gracefully danced about the interstate. It rested on a tandem triple-axle trailer with a goose-neck hitch tied into the bed of a brand new heavy-duty pickup truck. A work of art and masterpiece if there ever were one.

"No, Son," I sighed. "We can't get a boat like that."

"Thank you," Lynn said.

"Why not?" Tyler asked.

"Well, look at how big it is. First, we'll need to buy a truck big enough to pull it. It'll probably need a dually."

"What!" Lynn said. "Can't you remember anything!"

"What's a dually?" Tyler asked.

"It's a truck with four wheels on the back instead of just two. It usually comes on trucks with heavy-duty suspensions and is used to pull goose-neck trailers."

"Goose-neck?" he asked.

"Stop with all this nonsense!" Lynn said. "Nobody is getting a goose-neck boat or a dually trailer or anything related to a boat."

"I think you're a little confused," I said.

"No. I'm not confused. You're getting Tyler's hopes up and he's going to be disappointed when I have to take your dually goose neck boat back to the dealership."

"I think what you meant to say was . . ."

"Just stop. And drive."

It was clear the boat discussion had struck a nerve and perhaps created some hormonal imbalance—her emotional reaction and lack of coherency being the primary evidence. Relying on my years of experience in dealing with this type of situation, I remained calm and quiet, casually passing other cars so I could get directly behind the great white masterpiece. I figured she would come to her senses when given the opportunity to observe the fine art up close.

And oh was it beautiful! The three stainless steel props sparkled in the sunlight as the stern swayed back and forth on the road. It was nothing short of hypnotizing. Out of the corner of my eye, I noticed Lynn looking out the side window, no doubt an unconscious effort to resist the spell. I eased on the accelerator, switched lanes, and pulled alongside the boat. I eased our van up to the bow and then slowed to the stern. I did this again and again, sweeping alongside it like a paintbrush so Lynn could fully absorb the beauty of it all.

Out of the corner of my eye, I saw her glaring at me.

"What?" I asked.

"Go. Faster," she said.

"The speed limit is sixty-five here, I don't want to risk getting in a wreck or something."

Her lips began to quiver.

"You're going forty-five. Go faster now."

"Dad," Tyler said, "why are all those cars behind us honking their horns?"

"I don't know, Son. But we should let them pass. Let this be a lesson to you—always keep your eyes open for other drivers. They'll let anyone behind the wheel of a car these days."

I slowed down to get behind the boat and let the others pass.

"Safety first," I said, looking at Lynn.

Lynn sat in complete silence. This scared me.

Yet again, I leaned on my brain power to ease the tensions, remarking, "The weather sure is nice today."

Silence.

"I wonder if that family ahead of us is going to spend it on the water."

Silence.

The weather was nice. We were on day two of our road trip and were passing through the middle of South Carolina. I looked at the temperature gauge on the van.

"The temperature is seventy-five degrees outside," I said.

"Say that again?" Lynn asked.

"Seventy-five degrees. That's the temperature outside."

"It was thirty-seven when we left Rhode Island."

"I know," I said, removing a coat I still had on.

"Look at that exit. It's for Sandy Pines," Lynn said. "Kids, that is where your daddy grew up."

"Can we go there?" Tyler asked.

"Yes, but not today. We're heading to Savannah."

"Do Granddaddy and Grandmommy still live in Sandy Pines?"

"Yes, they do."

"I want to go!" Tyler said.

"Not today. We need to get moved in first."

Passing by the exit sign brought back a flood of memories I had long forgotten. They all took place in warm weather, on green grass, and under blue skies. Suddenly, a small, yellow beat-up truck interrupted my dreams. It raced from the Sandy Pines exit and almost ran us off the road.

"C'mon!" I said. "They are going to kill somebody!"

"I'll be glad to get off of this road and get to Danny's," Lynn said. "Did you have a lot of bugs in Sandy Pines?"

"No. Not that I can remember anyway. Why do you ask?"

"I don't know, I just recall Danny talking about some sort of biting fly in Savannah."

"Danny doesn't know anything about biting flies. He sells cars and doesn't know anything about anything except selling cars."

"I think he's doing very well at it," Lynn said.

"Exactly. That's why you can't trust what he says."

"I don't know," Lynn said. "He did offer you a job working for him. That was generous of him."

"There's no way I'll work for Danny. I'll go broke before I do that."

"Well, if you think about it . . ."

"I'm not going to think about it. Thinking about things just gets you in trouble. I'm not working for Danny."

Danny married my sister a few years back. I might have trusted Danny, but I knew better. We had grown up together as childhood friends. I was the only friend that lasted. And he all but ruined that by marrying my sister. Now, being friends was no longer a choice. He was family.

I drove on, still following the boat, but I could no longer appreciate its beauty. My mind raced on, thinking of ways I could earn money without working for Danny. There were many jobs better than working for Danny—working manual labor at a toxic waste site, cleaning sewers, or worse, being a middle manager for a large corporation. You name it. I would do it, so long as it meant not working for Danny.

The explosion woke baby girl up. Lynn screamed and Tyler said something about bombs going off around us. I casually eased into the left lane as shrapnel bounced off the windshield. Sparks flew in all directions and the boat immediately burst into flames. The truck pulling the boat slammed on its brakes and pulled off the road. In my rearview mirror, I saw a man and a woman dash to pull their children out of the crew cab of the truck. After I was convinced everyone behind me was alive, I sped away.

"Looks like they got a flat tire," I said.

"The entire boat was on fire!" Lynn said.

"Just a few sparks maybe," I said. "Nothing a body shop can't fix."

"The family was running away from flames!"

"Precautionary measures."

"We are never, ever getting a boat."

The drive could not get any worse. And it didn't. In fact, the weather seemed better and better as we neared Savannah.

We were driving to my sister's house first because we were one day ahead of the moving truck and needed a place to stay.

"Three hours left and we'll be there," I said, trying to inspire some amount of enthusiasm.

"Are we going to our new house?" Tyler asked.

"Not today. We are going to stay at Aunt Wendy Ann's tonight."

"Will Uncle Danny be there?"

"Unfortunately, yes."

"Hooray!"

"Don't be that way," Lynn said to me. "Danny and Wendy Ann have been very kind to us. They said we could stay with them as long as we needed to, and I think we should do just that. It will take us weeks or months to get our house repaired."

"Weeks or months! We'll be lucky if I can stay at Danny's for a day."

"I hear their house is really nice and it's on the water."

"If I know Danny, and I do, then their house will be nasty and in complete disrepair. He is allergic to work. He has never done a single chore in his life. I know this to be a fact. He would climb up a greased flagpole backward just to get away from work. I promise, you don't want to stay there."

In the next three hours, I kept watching the temperature rise, taking layers of clothing off until I had nothing on but a pair of shorts and a tee shirt. When we reached the Savannah exit, I replaced my shoes with flip-flops. The act was largely ceremonial, but it mattered to me. I was ready for a change.

"Hey, there's that yellow pickup truck again," Lynn said. "That's the one that pulled out in front of us at the Sandy Pines exit."

"No kidding," I said, thinking nothing of it at the time.

We drove through Savannah, following the directions Danny had sent us, finally arriving at the end of a road on one of Savannah's island neighborhoods. The entrance to his driveway was overgrown with vines and bushes. It was so thick that sight could not penetrate the leafy wall. The opening to the driveway was just big enough for a car. It was as if someone, probably Danny, had cut a path through the jungle with a jeep and then boarded up the hole with two old barn doors.

"Hah!" I said. "This is Danny's place all right. I'll get out and see if I can find a way in. It's too bad my chainsaw is on the moving truck."

Before I could open my van door, the two barn doors parted. Ahead of us lay a long white limestone driveway, flanked with orange trees and lemon trees and magnolia trees until you approached a tunnel of huge live oaks. Sunlight bounced off the perfectly manicured green grass. Birds bathed in magnificent water fountains the size of swimming pools. Off in the distance, ducks and geese floated about in a pond. This went on for what seemed like a mile until we rolled to a stop at the foot of a large white mansion. On the other side, I could see forever across the marsh.

We sat still in the van, stunned, as the front door of the house opened.

"Uncle Danny!" Tyler yelled.

There stood Danny, dressed in blue jeans and a long-sleeve shirt, grinning like an idiot.

"This must be some kind of trick," I said. "I bet Danny conned some rich person into letting him house sit for the weekend. You stay put and I'll see what is going on."

When I got out, the first thing I noticed was how perfect the weather was—a cool seventy-nine degrees, a light breeze, no humidity, blue skies, and in short exactly the paradise I had dreamed of. I became so overwhelmed by the perfectness that I thought I might even shake Danny's hand.

I looked back at Lynn and waved for them to come on out.

On the third step toward him, I felt the first one strike. Then another. And another. And another.

"What the bleep!" I said.

"Get back in the van, kids!" I heard Lynn say.

The stings came from every direction, but I could not see anything.

"Danny . . . bleep . . . must . . . bleep . . . have some kind of bleeping electrical fence. Bleep. Or something!"

"Danny!" I yelled. "Turn off your bleeping fence!"

I frantically began dancing and bleeping, involuntarily waving my legs and arms in every direction.

"Nice moves!" he yelled back. "I didn't know you would be that excited to see me, man."

"Mommy?" I heard Tyler say. "Why is Daddy dancing like that?"

"He's not dancing. Stay in the car."

"Mommy?"

"Yes?"

"What is a bleeping bleep of a bleep?"

"It's something you should never, ever say."

Lynn never used that type of language and I tried to reserve it only for necessary times. This was one of them.

"Hey, man," Danny said. "You ok?"

"No."

"Hah, looks like the no-see-ums got you."

"What!" I said while trying to land a triple axel on one foot.

Then I noticed the hundreds of welts on my legs.

"Hey, man. I think you need to get that checked out," Danny said.

I looked at Danny, trying to come up with some response while my brain wrestled with the onslaught of pain. Then the sky turned darker.

"Hey, man. Something's wrong with your eyeballs. It looks like they're being swallowed by your forehead."

I turned around and looked at Lynn. She sat there with her mouth wide open.

"Mommy," Tyler said. "Why does Daddy's head look like a balloon?"

I stumbled toward the van. Then fell.

"Oh bleep!" I heard Lynn say.

Those were the last words I heard before all went dark.

## CHAPTER 8

## *Nero*

"Let's go," Mori said. "No time to talk about it. Just get in the truck and go."

"What's the big hurry, Mori?" Judd asked his dad.

"I said, let's go!"

"Look. I'm not going anywhere unless I know where we're going and why," Judd said.

"We ain't got time for this. I'll tell you later. Look, Son, I need your help. Trust me."

Judd's dad had never asked him for help. And he could not remember the last time he had called him Son.

"All right, *Dad*," Judd said, putting a sarcastic emphasis on Dad. His dad was the last person Judd would trust, but he went anyway.

While they were riding through the back roads of Sandy Pines, Judd asked, "So why are they after you this time?"

"That's none of your business. All you need to know is we're getting out of here. Fast. I need a change of scenery and I got us a job just over the state line."

"Job? You've never had a real job in your life."

"I ain't talking about no real job. You'll see when we get there. You can thank me later."

"Who is after you? The law or one of your friends?" Judd asked.

"I said that's none of your business. And it will be better for you if we keep it that way."

Judd and his dad sped onto the interstate in Mori's yellow, beat-up truck, almost running right into a van.

"Fools!" Mori said, shaking his fist.

CHAPTER 9

# *My Father*

In the darkness, I could see a light. It was far away at first, but seemed to get closer and closer. Then it faded away to almost nothing before getting brighter and brighter again. I felt myself reach out to the light. Then all of a sudden, the light blazed with great brilliance. I saw two figures. One was dressed in a white robe, standing at the right side of the other. The other stood in the center of the bright light, his arms stretched out toward the sky. Then he spoke. When I heard his voice, I knew I was looking at my father.

"Dad? Is that you?" I asked.

"I can't get this dang light switch to work!" he said, flailing his arms around and ranting about the room.

"Dad?"

"What ever happened to using a simple switch! Who needs all these knobs and buttons! We need a brain surgeon just to turn on the lights."

"Hello, maybe I can help," the man dressed in white said. "My name is Oliver Manning. I am the attending physician. Technically, I am an immunologist and not certified as a neurosurgeon, but I did complete my residency working with a specialist on neurological and cranial matters."

"Hello. Can anyone hear me?" I asked.

"Look, doc. He's alive!" Dad said.

"Hello, Mr. Scott. You're awake," Dr. Manning said. "How are you feeling?"

"Confused. Where am I? What happened?"

"You are in a hospital. It appears that you have experienced anaphylactic shock."

"A what?"

"It is an allergic reaction to an antigen, where a flood of chemicals can cause a sudden decrease in blood pressure and a decrease in your airway diameter such that your vital organs cannot obtain sufficient oxygen. All of this is brought on by an extreme induction of an immune response."

I just looked at him.

"What does that mean?" I asked.

"You almost died."

"Oh."

"And you're allergic to no-see-ums."

"Oh. No," I said.

"Is this your first allergic reaction to an insect bite?" he asked.

"Yes. We just arrived from Rhode Island. I don't think they have no-see-ums."

"Rhode Island? What a wonderful place," he said. "I used to spend summers in Newport while I was in medical school. It might be my favorite place in the world. Are you familiar with Newport?"

"Yes, the summers are nice. We lived in Newport for the past two years."

"Well," Dr. Manning said, "that's good to hear. I'm glad you're just visiting. I suggest that you return to Newport as soon as possible. This is peak season for no-see-ums. You will need to be careful just walking across our parking lot."

"Doc. I can't go back."

"Why not?"

"We bought a house here, outside of Savannah."

"For vacation?"

"No. For, uh, . . ."

"The kid bought a house without ever seeing it in a town he has never visited," Dad said. "And he thinks he is going to live here forever. He is impulsive and reckless, always has been. Doc, do you have a cure for that?"

"Dad!"

"You could have talked to me first. I grew up near here and would have told you to think twice, or at least once, about your decision. But no, you quit a stable job and drug your family down without any idea what you were getting in to."

"Is this true?" Dr. Manning asked.

"Every bit of it," Dad said.

"Well, sort of, some of it. In fact, pretty much all of it. But, doc, I have to make it work. I have invested a lot into this move."

"Invest!" Dad said. "You call spending money you don't have on things you don't need investing! You don't know anything about investing. If you would have listened to me . . ."

"Dad! Stop! Please. Besides, you invest your money in shoeboxes and glass jars. I don't need your advice to know that's a bad idea."

"I worked too hard for some stranger to lose my money. Judgment is coming for this economy and I'll be ready."

"I'm sorry, doctor," I said. "What can we do? We must do something."

"Hmmm," Dr. Manning said, thinking to himself. Then he opened a cabinet and pulled out a long brown box.

"This should help," Dr. Manning said.

"Look at that sword!" Dad said.

"This? It is an epinephrine syringe. It will help prevent anaphylactic shock. It is the best way to prevent another attack. This and bug spray."

"Doc, I'm really not good with needles," I said.

"Yeah, doc. He's never been that tough. It gets worse with each generation, I think."

Dr. Manning pulled another syringe from the box.

"This one is to practice with," he said.

"A practice needle?"

"Yes, it is important that you and your loved ones know how to use it in case of an emergency. Is your wife here in the hospital?"

"My wife? Yes, where is Lynn?"

"She went with your mother," Dad said. "They said something about shopping for some type of clothes, eternity or maternity or something. Must be some foreign brand. I've never heard of it. It sounded like they were talking about underwear so I stayed out of it."

"I'll need to train someone how to use it before you're discharged."

"Hey, doc, let me hold it please," Dad said.

"Dad. Stay away from me with that thing!"

"Relax, kid," Dad said. "It's just a practice needle. Doc? Is this how it works?" he said, easing it toward my leg.

"Dad! Stop!"

"No. No," Dr. Manning said, taking the syringe from my dad.

"Thanks, doc," I said. "He is old and crazy. Do you see what I have had to deal with all these years?"

"Never do that," Dr. Manning said. "This is a spring-operated syringe with a pressure-operated trigger mechanism. The spring propels the needle on contact. Like this."

I did not have time to move. In a flash, Dr. Manning slammed the syringe into my thigh.

"Holy bleep!" Dad said.

I screamed like a little child and felt my leg go numb.

"See, that wasn't so bad," Dr. Manning said.

"Doc, I think it was so bad," Dad said. "Look at him."

The numbness spread to the rest of my body. Again, I could not breathe and felt myself begin to go.

"Doc!" Dad said. "He's about to faint!"

"Doc!" I said. "I can't feel anything! I'm about to go."

Again, my world turned dark. It was back to the tunnel and the light and the voices for me.

"He will be ok," Dr. Manning said. "There is no needle on the practice syringe."

"Really?" Dad said.

"Really?" I said, crawling back from the horror.

"You can't feel anything because nothing happened. It was all in your mind."

"Oh."

"I told you he was a wimp," Dad said, laughing.

"I'm sorry, doctor. These near-death experiences are getting annoying."

"What did you call me?" Dad said.

"Nothing. I said . . ."

"There is no need to worry," Dr. Manning continued. "This is just a practice syringe. An actual injection from the real syringe would be very painful."

"Let me see that thing," Dad said, picking up the real needle by accident and touching it with his index finger.

"Wait!" Dr. Manning said.

From the check-in desk, Mom and Lynn heard the screams and crashing of tables.

"Oh dear!" Mom said. "It sounds like a couple of young children are fighting in one of the recovery rooms. I hope their parents are nearby."

"Tyler," Lynn said. "Let this be a lesson to you and your sister. Never fight, especially in a hospital. It is wrong and can disturb people who need peace and quiet the most. Come quickly. Let's go check on your father."

"Lynn," Mom said as she neared our room. "I think those children are in Mel's room."

"Oh my. They must have moved him out already. How long have we been shopping?"

Right before they walked in, Dad had fallen to the ground in pain. Dr. Manning tried to keep him still while I tried to wrestle the needle away from his finger.

"Hold his arms down!" Dr. Manning said.

"Mothershuckinbitfartinsonofuhshasstuckerhore . . . [censored]," Dad unleashed a stream of obscenities that, if decipherable, would have shocked the conscience of all mankind.

"Granddaddy?" Tyler said, walking in with Lynn.

"Quick. Hold his arms down!" Dr. Manning said.

Running off a spike of adrenaline, I lunged at Dad. With all my strength, I pulled the needle from Dad's finger.

"Got it!" I said.

"You two should be ashamed of yourselves!" Mom said. "We can't leave you alone for a few minutes without you getting into a fight. And in a hospital. Someone could get hurt."

"There is a hole in my finger," Dad said.

"I almost died," I added.

"Both of you need to act like adults for once. This behavior is not acceptable."

"Hello, ma'am," Dr. Manning said to my mom. "I'm Dr. Manning. Is this your husband?"

"Yes."

"He just penetrated his right index digit with a syringe full of epinephrine."

"Did you say he broke one of your medical instruments? Well, we will have it fixed. I am so ashamed that he has behaved this way."

"Ma'am, he was lucky. The needle went all the way through his finger."

"Lucky!" Dad said.

"Yes," Dr. Manning said. "None of the dosage entered your bloodstream."

"Say that again, please," Mom said.

"Dad stuck himself with a big needle," I said.

"Oh," Mom said.

"It really is amazing," Dr. Manning said. "Because of the cylindrical shape, sudden impact, and sharpness of the needle, it should heal nicely."

"Can I see it?" Tyler asked.

"No," Lynn said. "We have had enough excitement for the day."

"It is good to see you, honey," I said.

"It is time for us to go," Lynn said. "The moving truck arrived yesterday."

"The doctor said I am doing better now," I said.

"There are boxes everywhere," Lynn said. "In the garage. Outside of the garage. In the front yard."

"He said my airways shut down. Anaphylactic shock or something."

"It is probably going to rain this evening, so we can't waste any time."

"Another bite from a no-see-um and the same thing will happen."

"I can only imagine what the neighbors are thinking."

I gave Tyler a hug and then tapped Lynn on her shoulder, just to make sure she knew I was ok and that I understood if the whole ordeal made her emotional and that I was in the room standing next to her.

"Well," she said, "I am glad you finally woke up from your little nap. We have a lot of work to do."

"Doctor?" I asked. "When can I be discharged?"

"Right away. In fact, I doubt your insurance will cover another night. The last thing you want is to pay full price for a night in the hospital."

"Lynn," I said. "Can you take Tyler and Sophia to the van? I'll be right down."

"Yes, of course. Please hurry up."

Mom and Lynn and the kids left for the van.

"Doc," I said. "About insurance?"

"Yes."

"Well. I don't have any."

"Oh."

"I can't believe it," Dad said. "Actually, I can. You'll never learn, will you, kid? Like I said, doctor. Reckless and impulsive."

"Dad. Enough."

"Hmmm," Dr. Manning said to himself. "The hospital has a strict billing policy. These syringes alone are $700 without insurance."

"There must be something we can do."

"Let me see," Dr. Manning said, looking through a cabinet.

"How many children do you have?" he asked.

"Two. Five years old and two years old."

"And another on the way?"

"Yes."

"What was that?" Dad asked.

"Your wife is about two months along, right?" Dr. Manning asked.

"Yes. How did you know?"

"I am a doctor. I notice things like that."

"Lynn is pregnant?" Dad asked.

"Take this," Dr. Manning said, handing me a syringe. "There will not be a charge. It is part of my in-house supply."

"Thank you," I said.

"Another child," Dad said. "Son, you've really outdone yourself this time."

"It sounds like you're about to have a full house," Dr. Manning said. "I know it is tough being a parent. Here is my card. It has my cell on it. Feel free to call if you have any questions. I don't mind at all, especially if it is one of those situations where you don't know if you need to go to the ER or not."

"Thank you," I said.

"He's going to need that, doc," Dad said. "He went to the hospital five times before he was five."

"That's because no one was watching me," I said.

"I was working. Your mom was there."

"She locked us out of the house."

"Fresh air is good for children."

"Not for toddlers."

"It's called teaching children to think for themselves."

"It's called child neglect! People don't do that anymore."

"Humph. I can tell when I'm not needed," Dad said. "I'm going to the car."

"Finally," I said as Dad got his bag and walked to the door.

He turned and looked at me before he left. "Son," he said. "I'm the oldest Scott alive. When it comes to life spans, we don't have a good average. Try not to make it worse." And he left.

"Doc, thank you for everything. What's the next step?"

"Unfortunately, almost all of the follow-up tests must be approved by your insurance company first. And hospital policy prohibits us from circumventing these rules. I will see what I can do."

On the way out, we ran into Mom.

"Did Dad find you?"

"Yes. He is with Lynn and the kids. I came to help you get discharged."

"Thank you, Mom. I'm sorry for the commotion. Sometimes Dad is very difficult to get along with."

"He would not want me to tell you this, but it was his idea to come here," Mom said. "He dropped everything, immediately. He got in the truck and drove straight here. And he has been sitting in your hospital room for two days and has not left until just now."

"Two days? I've been in here for two days?"

"Yes."

"Well, maybe I was a little hard on him," I said.

"I'll take you to the check-out desk," Dr. Manning said. "We'll see what we can do about the bill. Probably nothing. But we'll see."

"Ok."

We gathered all of our belongings and followed Dr. Manning to the desk.

"Mr. Scott is ready for discharge," he told the clerk. "Unfortunately, he does not have any insurance. I understand the hospital's policy on billing. Is there anything we can do to delay when payment is due?"

"For Mr. Scott?"

"Yes."

"That's not necessary."

"Why?"

"There is no balance."

"That must be a mistake," I said.

"No. I am certain it is not. Just a few minutes ago, a man paid for everything. In cash. He pulled it right out of a shoebox. I've never seen that before."

CHAPTER 10

# A Day of Preparation

Saturday had always been a day of preparation for Pastor David, but this Saturday was like no other. It was a special Sabbath. It was Saturday, a time to worship. It was the Passover, a time to reflect. It was the day before Easter, a time to rejoice. There was much to do.

This Saturday, the traditions of Pastor David collided with those of Rabbi David. He believed there was no incompatibility in these traditions and that they were merged just as the Old Testament was merged with the New Testament to form the Holy Bible. While Pastor David remained loyal to both traditions, he wondered when and why the rest of the world had separated the old from the new.

He prepared the cups of wines. He bookmarked the verses of the Passover story. He prepared the bread. He found his traditional blessings. He prepared the table. Preparation of the meal came last. He wanted to make sure all was complete before he prepared the meal.

It was noon when Pastor David began preparing the meal. The meal was a lamb. For thousands and thousands of years, it had been a lamb. It had always been a lamb. Pastor David, when preparing the Passover meal, took great care when preparing the lamb. Like every other year, he struggled when preparing the lamb. But this year was different. He did not know why. Maybe it was because of the convergence of Passover and Easter and all of the traditions he loved so much. Maybe it was something else. But Pastor David wept when he prepared the lamb. He wept like he had never wept before. He was not the kind of man who wept often. He was strong. He was a man of reason. He was a man of logic. He was not a man who let emotions overcome him. But he wept when he prepared the lamb.

Perhaps it was the Gospel of John. He had been studying John in preparation of Easter Sunday.

His church had grown and Easter was the biggest day of the year. True to his nature, Pastor David had anticipated the growth in the church and had hired an associate pastor, Pastor Andrew.

Pastor David had asked Pastor Andrew to deliver the main sermon. This allowed Pastor David to prepare for the Scripture readings while Pastor Andrew prepared the main sermon. This provided some relief to Pastor David during this very busy time of year. Pastor David, therefore, put his full energy into the Scripture readings—a first reading before the main sermon and a second reading after the main sermon. The second reading would precede Holy Communion and include passages from the Gospel of John.

Pastor David felt the need to provide his congregation with a very precise account of how Jesus was crucified. The details were important to him. He would keep it short and to the point, with little interpretation. He wanted his congregation to see the text as it was written thousands of years ago.

Pastor David would start with the day Jesus was tried and crucified. He found the verse he was looking for.

"Then they took Jesus from Caiaphas to Pilate's headquarters. It was early in the morning. They themselves did not enter the headquarters, so as to avoid ritual defilement and to be able to eat the Passover."

Pastor David placed a mark on John 18:28.

Ah, this must explain why I have wept so while preparing the Passover meal, he thought. Jesus was tried during the morning before the Passover meal. It makes perfect sense now.

Pastor David continued to read.

"Now it was the day of Preparation for the Passover; and it was about noon. He said to the Jews, 'Here is your King!' They cried out, 'Away with him! Away with him! Crucify him!' Pilate asked them, 'Shall I crucify your King?' The chief priests answered, 'We have no king but the emperor.' Then he handed him over to them to be crucified."

He marked John 19:14.

Yes, it all made sense now. This brought great relief to Pastor David. He knew now why he had wept so. His faith was speaking to him and guiding him to this Scripture. This was the perfect Scripture for this Easter Sunday, when the two traditions merged. This was the perfect Scripture for Pastor David because it showed a level of detail that might be lost on another pastor.

Pastor David thought, I will tell them how I wept today while preparing the Passover lamb. I will share with them how I did not realize why I had wept. I will explain that I began preparing the Passover meal at noon, the time of day when Pilate handed Jesus over to be crucified. I will explain that Jesus had been tried and crucified on the day when

Jews were preparing for the Passover meal. I will explain that it is a Jewish tradition to sacrifice a lamb that day.

Pastor David continued his reading of John, confident he would find the proper text to end his reading before Holy Communion. And he found it.

"When Jesus saw his mother and the disciple whom he loved standing beside her, he said to his mother, 'Woman, here is your son.' Then he said to the disciple, 'Here is your mother.' And from that hour the disciple took her into his own home. After this, when Jesus knew that all was now finished, he said (in order to fulfill the scripture), 'I am thirsty.' A jar full of sour wine was standing there. So they put a sponge full of wine on a branch of hyssop and held it to his mouth. When Jesus had received the wine, he said, 'It is finished.' Then he bowed his head and gave up his spirit. Since it was the day of Preparation, the Jews did not want the bodies left on the cross during the Sabbath, especially because that Sabbath was a day of great solemnity."

He marked John 19:26-31.

It was perfect, he thought. It was the message his congregation needed to hear, one with accuracy and clarity. He would show them that this most important moment, the death of Jesus, was recorded with precision, to the day and to the hour. In the morning on the day of preparation for the Passover, the Lamb was tried. At noon, He was handed over to be crucified. That afternoon, the Lamb was killed.

Pastor David's faith had never felt stronger. He prayed a prayer of thanks for guiding him to this Scripture. He prayed a prayer of thanks for giving him the Scripture to guide him and instruct him. He prayed a prayer of commitment that he would share this experience with his congregation. He prayed a prayer of hope that they too would find confidence and assurance in the Word of God.

At the end of his prayer, he knew immediately what he must read to the congregation during the first Scripture reading, before the main sermon.

He would start the first reading with Scripture from the very end of the Bible.

"I warn everyone who hears the words of the prophecy of this book; if anyone adds to them, God will add to that person the plagues described in this book; if anyone takes away from the words of the book of this prophecy, God will take away that person's share in the tree of life and in the holy city, which are described in this book."

He put a note at the end of Revelations.

Pastor David would read this with confidence and authority. He would tell them to have faith in the Word of God. He would remind them that the Holy Scripture is the inerrant Word of God. He would remind them that the Word of God is infallible. He would remind them that it has remained true and accurate for thousands of years, despite tremendous efforts to prove otherwise.

He would conclude by reading verses from Proverbs. He found two of his favorite verses, Proverbs 30:5-6, and marked them.

"Every word of God proves true; he is a shield to those who take refuge in him. Do not add to his words, or else he will rebuke you, and you will be found a liar."

He was prepared and ready now. He knew it was a strong message, but one that must be delivered. It all made sense to him, tying readings from the Old and New Testaments to show that the message has survived the test of time. He knew this was his duty and he was pleased.

CHAPTER 11

# *The Marina*

"I'll ride with Dad," I said.

"Ok. We'll go to the house and start unpacking. Do you know how to get there?" Lynn asked.

"Sure. I got it."

"Because there is no cell service out there. You will not be able to call if you get lost."

"Fine. Just go. I spent almost a decade in the military. I can read a map."

"All right. We'll see you soon."

I got in Dad's truck.

"It looks like the ladies are in a hurry," I said to him. "Can I ride with you?"

"Sure. You know where to go?" Dad asked.

"Sure."

We left the hospital and rode toward the interstate and then to a small town near Savannah and then through the small town, where the road narrowed. We rode for miles and miles without seeing a house or car.

"Do you have directions?" he asked.

"In my head," I said.

"So, tell me, where in your head is the middle of nowhere?"

"We still have a ways. Lynn said we were out there."

"Out there! We were out there twenty minutes ago. We have already driven to the middle of nowhere. Now we are going past it."

"She said to drive down this road until it almost ends and then take a left."

"Well, I don't think this road ends," he said.

"Or maybe it was a right," I said.

"I don't understand why you would buy a house you've never seen in a place you've never visited."

"It looked good on a map."

"There's nothing but pine trees out here."

"I had a hefty bill at the hospital, Dad."

"Yeah?"

"I tried to pay it, but they would not let me."

"You can't pay for something unless you have money to pay for it."

"I have a credit card."

"A credit card. That is nothing but trouble. If you don't have the money, you shouldn't buy it," Dad said.

"They said some angry old man paid my bill."

"Humph."

"With cash, right from a shoebox."

"Well, I didn't see any angry men at the hospital," Dad said.

"Yeah, maybe he was just old," I said.

We drove and drove with nothing but forests around us.

"How do you expect to raise kids and make a living way out here in the woods?" Dad asked.

"Lynn said we are in a neighborhood. I'll make it work. You'll see."

We kept driving.

"Mom said I was out for two days," I said.

"Seemed longer," Dad said.

"I guess the local hotels were booked."

"Too expensive."

"Dr. Manning seemed like a good man," I said.

"Don't lose his number. You'll need to pack a lunch just to drive to the hospital."

"Here's our turn."

Dad turned left, where the pavement ended. The truck bumped and rattled down an old road. Ahead of us stood a tunnel of oak limbs reaching out from massive trunks.

"Maybe we should have turned right," I said.

The road ended at a large, old white house. Much of the paint was chipped. Seven brick chimneys extended through the roof. Around the large house were small houses, all white and chipped. The large house sat on a bluff overlooking a sea of marsh grass.

"There ain't no neighborhood here," Dad said.

"Let's turn around," I said.

"Just a minute," Dad said, parking the car. "Let's check it out."

I was wearing blue jeans and long sleeves and all my skin was covered with bug spray. We walked to the edge of the bluff. To the right sat a small concrete building.

"That's tabby," Dad said.

"Tabby?"

"Made from oyster shells. Even the mortar has ground-up oyster shells. Spanish used it."

"Spanish?"

"Yeah, about five-hundred years ago."

Far ahead of us, the horizon met the marsh grass. There were islands scattered about the vast marsh. Creeks and rivers zigzagged through the marsh on their way to the ocean.

"I haven't seen a tabby house since I was a boy," Dad said. "I spent a lot of time on this water, not too far from here."

We walked to the edge of the tall bluff. Below us rested a long makeshift dock, with plastic fifty-gallon barrels for floats. It was packed with houses and old boats. The houses floated up and down with the dock and the boats.

"Is that your neighborhood?" Dad asked.

"No."

"Too bad. I always wanted to live on a boat."

"Really? I never knew that."

"It was my plan to buy a trawler and live on it, but your mom wouldn't go for it."

"Why not?" I asked.

"Because she is smarter than I am, that's why."

"I understand."

A wooden ramp connected the bluff to the neighborhood of floating houses. A man stood on the bluff near the ramp. He waved as if he knew us.

"Hello," the man said, walking toward us. He was clean-cut and clean-shaven. He wore khaki pants with a perfect crease down the middle. There were no wrinkles on his white, collared shirt.

"I don't believe we have met. I'm David," the man said.

"Hello, I'm Mel. We just moved here."

"To the marina?" He asked.

"No, just to the area," I said. "In fact, we took a wrong turn and ended up here. I'm looking for Rumble Road."

"Rumble Road! That is where I live. Just go back the way you came. It is the first road on your left, leaving the marina."

"So, it's close?" I asked.

"Very close," he said.

"This view is amazing," I said.

"Yes, it is. You know, people spend thousands of dollars to go on vacation just north of us at Hilton Head. You and I can do this for free."

"I heard the bugs were bad down here," I said, looking around.

"Yes. The no-see-ums are deadly, but this breeze keeps them away. And stay in the sunshine, otherwise, they will carry you off."

"How long have you lived here?" I asked.

"About ten years now."

"What brought you here?"

"I am a pastor and this might sound unusual, but I felt called to come here. I had never seen the place."

"I see."

"I don't know what your religious affiliation is, if any," he said. "But you are welcome to join us at church. It is the first one on the right, heading back into town."

"Thank you," I said. "Maybe we will see you around."

"You will. Rumble Road is a small community. It was a pleasure meeting you."

Dad and I got in the truck and drove back. The first road we found was Rumble Road. We drove around a bend in the road and the forest opened up to a neighborhood.

"Here it is," I said.

We drove down the road at a slow pace, taking it all in until we found my house. We pulled into the driveway and stopped. It was an old house but new to me. It was my first house. No more renting small apartments. I now owned a house. I thought about all the exciting projects ahead. It was something to look forward to. Lynn and Mom were busy unpacking boxes. They waved and Lynn smiled. We had arrived.

CHAPTER 12

## *When Jesus Died*

He has risen!
It was the first thought in Pastor David's mind when he awoke on Easter morning.
He has risen!

No other day brought more joy to Pastor David than Easter. It was this moment in ancient history that brought meaning and purpose to his life.

He has risen!

The night before, Pastor David had laid out his clothes and his Bible and his prepared Scripture readings. Everything was in place and ready for the day. He ate his oatmeal and tended to a few matters before leaving for Sunday service.

At church, he greeted members of the congregation at the door. All were in good spirits. The entire church beamed with joy and energy. Even the weather seemed to rejoice.

The service began with a recitation of the Nicene Creed. The creed had served him well over the years. After reciting it with the congregation, he repeated a portion to himself.

*For our sake he was crucified under Pontius Pilate;*
*he suffered death and was buried.*
*On the third day he rose again*
*in accordance with the Scriptures . . . .*

It was this passage that carried special weight today. Through His death, we are saved, Pastor David said to himself. Pastor David prayed a prayer of thanks. He gave thanks for salvation and for the Scriptures that told us and continued to tell us what happened the day that Jesus died.

Soon the time came for Pastor David to deliver his first Scripture reading. With power and passion and authority, he told the congregation that the Word of God is true and inerrant and infallible and the source of all that is worthy.

As planned, he cited Revelations, booming a recitation of the Scripture, "I warn everyone who hears the words of the prophecy of this book; if anyone adds to them, God will add to that person the plagues described in this book; if anyone takes away from the words of the book of this prophecy, God will take away that person's share in the tree of life and in the holy city, which are described in this book."

He cited Proverbs, again booming the Scripture, "Every word of God proves true; he is a shield to those who take refuge in him. Do not add to his words, or else he will rebuke you, and you will be found a liar!"

Then he paused. A long pause.

Not one member, not even a child who knew no better, dared make a noise. Something in Pastor David's voice that morning struck a powerful and mesmerizing tone. He spoke with a rhythm and a cadence that was uncustomary to his traditional ways. He himself did not expect such a passionate delivery.

At the end of the first reading, he concluded in a more somber tone, "Ladies and Gentlemen. My friends. We put our trust and faith in the Scriptures. We put our trust and faith in this day, Easter Sunday. Let us be thankful for it and for those who have kept our faith alive these thousands of years. For thousands of years, people have tried to prove the Scriptures wrong. But it cannot be done. The Bible is the Word of God and therefore flawless. Let us ask God to help us spread the Good News in the Scriptures so that others might be saved."

"Amen," the congregation said in unison.

It was Pastor Andrew's turn.

"Ladies and Gentlemen," Pastor Andrew said. "He has risen!"

"Amen!" echoed the congregation.

"Today is a wonderful day. Not just because the sun is shining and the birds are out and winter is behind us, but because today we get to celebrate the death and resurrection of Jesus Christ our Savior."

"Amen!" echoed the congregation.

"And I am especially honored this morning because Pastor David asked me to deliver the sermon. He, like everyone here, has welcomed me to this church. For that, I am grateful."

Pastor Andrew paused and then continued, "As I listened to Pastor David's Scripture reading, I thought, wow! What a perfect and powerful message. It was as if he and I had worked together to prepare the Scripture readings and the sermon. The only explanation is that the Holy Spirit was with us both this week. Too often, I take the Scripture for granted. I sometimes fail to look at the detail that it provides. I fail to see that these details are gifts. But think about it for a moment. What would we do without the Scripture? How would we know that Jesus died for our sins thousands of years ago? Ladies and Gentlemen, the Scripture is our guide. It is our instruction manual on life. And it is more than that. It is a historical record that tells us exactly what happened to Jesus more than two thousand years ago. This morning, I want to focus the sermon on what the Scripture tells us about the first Easter, when Jesus died. And I will read the text exactly from the Scripture so you can see the detail the Scripture provides. Ladies and Gentlemen, the details are important. The details give us confidence in the Word and in knowing exactly what happened when Jesus died."

Pastor David sat amazed. This was exactly the same message he wanted to deliver, yet he had not discussed this at all with Pastor Andrew.

Pastor Andrew continued, "When something important happens to someone in our lives, especially if that someone is a loved one, we want to know all the details about what happened, right? Especially if we were not there. After the birth of a child, it is customary to send the name of the newborn, the time of birth, and the weight. These details are important. If one of your children were injured and you were not there to see it, you would want to know all the details, right? The time and place of the injury. How the injury happened, right? Just imagine if one of your loved ones was killed. You would want to know how he or she was killed and make sure that all the details were recorded, right? Well, that is what happened with Jesus. And we are his loved ones. And we are blessed with an accurate accounting of what happened the day Jesus died. Let us look at the Scriptures."

Pastor Andrew continued, "Before Jesus was crucified, Jesus told Peter, his faithful follower: 'Truly I tell you, this day, this very night, before the cock crows twice, you will deny me three times. But Peter said vehemently, 'even though I must die with you, I will not deny you.' And all of them said the same."

Pastor David recalled that message very well and that Peter wasted no time in denying Jesus, just as Jesus had predicted.

"And we all know what happened next," Pastor Andrew said. "Jesus was given to Pontius Pilate. The Bible tells us exactly what happens next: 'Pilate spoke to them again, 'Then what do you wish me to do with the man you call the King of the Jews?' They shouted back, 'Crucify him.'"

Yes, this is exactly what happened, Pastor David recalled, pleased with Pastor Andrew's approach and dedication to the details.

Remembering the verse he had marked, Pastor David recalled that Pilate handed Jesus over to the Jews at noon.

"Pilate handed Jesus to the Jews before nine o'clock in the morning," Pastor Andrew said.

"No. No," Pastor David said to himself. It was at noon. I'm sure of it. The Scripture said it happened at noon. Pastor David flipped through his notes and found the verse—John 19:14. There it was as plain as day that Pilate handed him over at noon. Oh dear, he thought. What a disaster. He hated to correct Pastor Andrew in front of the congregation, but it must be done. He must think of how to do so with tact and compassion and without embarrassing his colleague.

"And how do we know it was before nine o'clock in the morning?" Pastor Andrew said. "Because the Bible tells us so. Mark 15:25 states, 'It was nine o'clock in the morning when they crucified him.'"

"This cannot be true," Pastor David said to himself. Jesus was with Pilate at noon. He could not have been crucified at nine in the morning and been with Pilate. That is impossible.

Pastor Andrew continued, "When it was noon, darkness came over the whole land until three in the afternoon. At three o'clock Jesus cried out with a loud voice, 'Eloi, Eloi, lema sabachthani?' which means, 'My God, my God, why have you forsaken me?' We find this in Mark 15:33-34."

"No. No. No," Pastor David said to himself. Jesus was with Pilate at noon. He could not have been on the cross at noon.

Darkness came over Pastor David. He shook and shivered and tried to do his best to remain focused and methodical. He raced back and forth through verses he marked as Pastor Andrew continued.

"Then Jesus gave a loud cry and breathed his last," Pastor Andrew continued. "Ladies and Gentlemen. All this happened and Jesus knew it was going to happen. We know this because he told the disciples the night before—at the Last Supper. Can you imagine having dinner with your closest family and friends knowing that dinner would be your last meal with your loved ones? Can you imagine what it is like to look at your loved ones and tell them that tonight is our last night together and that tomorrow I will be tortured and I will die?"

Silence in the congregation.

Pastor Andrew continued, "My friends and family. That is exactly what happened the night before, at the Last Supper. And again, the Scripture tells us exactly what happened. Let us turn to Mark 14:12. It says, 'On the first day of Unleavened Bread, when the Passover lamb is sacrificed, his disciples said to him, 'where do you want us to go and make the preparations for you to eat the Passover?'"

Impossible! Pastor David thought. The Last Supper could not have been the Passover. Jesus died before the Passover meal was eaten, not after. This is all wrong. Jesus could not have eaten the sacrificial lamb at Passover. Jesus was the lamb! Jesus died before the Passover meal was eaten, slaughtered like all the other lambs!

Pastor Andrew continued, "Ladies and Gentlemen. The Last Supper was more than just a last supper—it was the Passover, an ancient Jewish tradition."

No! This cannot be! Pastor David looked at the verses he had marked.

Pastor David looked at John 18:28. It read, "Then they took Jesus from Caiaphas to Pilate's headquarters. It was early in the morning. They themselves did not enter the headquarters, so as to avoid ritual defilement and to be able to eat the Passover."

He looked at John 19:14. It read, "Now it was the day of Preparation for the Passover; and it was about noon. He said to the Jews, 'Here is your King!' They cried out, 'Away with him! Away with him! Crucify him!' Pilate asked them, 'Shall I crucify your King?' The chief priests answered, 'We have no king but the emperor.' Then he handed him over to them to be crucified."

My faith rests on the death and resurrection of Jesus, Pastor David thought. My faith rests on the accuracy of the Bible. John wrote that Jesus was crucified before the Passover meal was eaten, but Mark wrote that Jesus was crucified after the Passover meal was eaten. How could this be? How could the Scriptures get this most important detail wrong? He had studied the Bible his entire life. How could he have missed this?

Pastor David looked again at the verses in Mark. Then he looked at the verses in John. Then at Mark. Then at John. Then at Mark. What if there was more he had missed? The thought of this was too much for him to bear. The world around Pastor David grew even darker. He went back and forth through his verses. Back and forth. Back and forth, hoping that he had missed something or misread something. He rocked back and forth. Back and forth, while Pastor Andrew continued. But Pastor David heard nothing.

Pastor Andrew had almost finished the sermon. Soon it would be Pastor David's turn to deliver his Scripture reading for Holy Communion. He was to read from the Gospel of John. He was to point out that Jesus died during the day before the Passover meal was eaten, while lambs were being sacrificed. He was going to point out that Jesus was the Lamb!

Pastor David rocked back and forth, staring straight ahead while Pastor Andrew concluded.

"When the Sabbath was over," Pastor Andrew said, "Mary Magdalene, and Mary the mother of James, and Salome bought spices, so that they might go and anoint him. And very early on the first day of the week, when the sun had risen, they went to the tomb. They had been saying to one another, 'Who will roll away the stone for us from the entrance to the tomb?' When they looked up, they saw that the stone, which was very large, had already been rolled back. As they entered the tomb, they saw a young man, dressed in a white robe, sitting on the right side, and they were alarmed. But he said to them, 'Do not be alarmed; you are looking for Jesus of Nazareth, who was crucified. He has been raised; he is not here. Look, there is the place they laid him. But go, tell his disciples and Peter that he is going ahead of you to Galilee; there you will see him, just as he told you.' So they went out and fled from the tomb, for terror and amazement had seized them; and they said nothing to anyone, for they were afraid."

Pastor David rocked back and forth, staring straight ahead. Everything around him had faded away. He rocked back and forth. In his pocket, he held tight to a stone—a red stone.

# PART TWO

## CHAPTER 13

# *My House*

It is disgusting to see what is on television these days. Preying on our fears and desensitizing society by constantly resetting what we accept as normal, companies stretch the boundaries of decency in search of shock value, all in the pursuit of higher profits. This comes at the expense of those who have experienced real trauma, and those fragile souls risk reliving their trauma almost anytime they watch a show on television.

"Turn it off! Turn it off!" I said.

"What is it? What happened?" Lynn asked.

"I can't watch it!" I said.

"Really?"

"Yes. Please."

"Maybe we can just watch another five minutes. It was just getting to the good part," Lynn said.

"No. No. Let me leave the room first."

"Ok."

I left the room.

The temptation was too much. There is something about fear and horror that draws one to it. I felt myself creep back into the living room to see what happened next.

"Um, I know you're there," Lynn said.

"Please turn it off. I can't watch, but I can't look away."

"Stop being so weird. It is a home improvement show. They are just taking out a wall to move some plumbing."

The thought of it alone caused me to break out into a sweat.

We had been in our house for almost a month, but it seemed like years, probably because of the slow and painful torture I had suffered at the hands of my house. From day one, my house had tried to kill me. It started with seemingly innocent electrical problems—most of the outlets did not work. Lights flickered. And I was hell-bent on fixing everything myself. This was in part due to my nature and in part due to being broke.

About a week prior to the most recent incident, I had joined Danny for lunch in downtown Savannah. He wanted to introduce me to a couple of friends, thinking they might help me find a job. I do not recall their names, but I remember the conversation moving quickly to the topic of houses.

"Like a lot of homes in Savannah, my home is Victorian," one of Danny's friends said. "I don't know if I would have chosen this style, but my wife fell in love with it at first sight."

"My house is a ranch-style house," the other friend said. "My husband picked it out. He wanted everything on one level. It works for us, but it just seems to go on forever. So, I guess it is more of a rambling ranch."

"Mel," Danny said. "I haven't seen your place yet. What kind of house do you own?"

I thought about it for a moment.

"My house is a bitch," I said.

"I beg your pardon?" the ranch-house lady said.

"Did I say that out loud?" I asked. "I'm so sorry. It's just that was the first word that came to mind. But it is an honest answer. I guess I should have said it's the kind of house that tries to kill you every time you try to do something else other than work on it."

Blank stares.

"Well. The food sure is good here," I said. "What is that outside? Is that a clown juggling fire?"

"Where?" they asked.

"I don't see it," the Victorian-house guy said.

"Maybe it was something else. Anyway, how's the weather?"

No job opportunities came from that lunch.

I recalled that conversation as I admired a patch of green grass in my backyard. I was proud of that patch of green grass. After $120 worth of fertilizer and countless hours of watering it by hand, it should look good. As long as I trained my eyes on the patch of grass and on that small patch of grass alone, the yard looked great. That was enough to give me a small dose of satisfaction.

It is important, I think, when you are struggling, to find small wins and savor them. That patch of grass was one of my wins.

Then it started to rain. I felt a soft drizzle on my face. Then the big drops came. Big heavy drops that precede a great downpour.

I found this odd because the sky was clear, not a cloud in the sky, and I was sitting in my favorite chair downstairs in our living room.

Lynn walked in the room and looked at me and then looked at the ceiling. Right about then, the drywall gave way and crumbled. Our living room turned into an indoor swimming pool.

"Hooray!" Tyler said, racing off to get his bathroom toys.

Tyler and Sophia were splashing and swimming about the living room, the water now ankle-deep. I had not yet mustered the energy to get out of my chair. My house had tormented me this way before and I did not want it to get the best of me again.

One of the problems with buying a house sight unseen is that you do not get to see that the house should be condemned. The thanks I got from my house for trying to save it was more pain and suffering. Our roof leaked every time it rained, just never in the same spot and never in places that humans can find. I learned how water could run down and up rafters. I learned how a single loose nail could lead to a raging river in my attic under just the right circumstances, those circumstances being any time it rained. I also learned that water rots wood. Rotten wood invites bugs. Bugs eat my house, which tries to kill me.

"Your floor is leaking," my mom said during one visit.

"That's impossible," I told her. "Water can't leak upwards. There's three feet of space between my floor and the ground."

"Well, it's leaking," she said. "And it's ruined the bathroom floors. You need to call a plumber."

"I'm not calling a plumber!" I said.

I donned on my usual hazmat gear and crawled under my house. No sign of water coming from the ground. But sure enough, the subfloor in the bathroom was soaking wet.

Maybe the tub is leaking, I thought. So I went back inside and looked for a leak.

"It looks like I'll need to open up the wall to see where the leak is coming from," I said.

After several hours of cutting drywall, I announced, "Good news. All the pipes and fittings going into this room are good. I'll go back under the house."

The subfloor was saturated now. Water was dripping from the subfloor. I ripped away a piece of insulation and immediately saw the problem.

I went back inside to announce the good news.

"I found it."

"Well, what is it?"

"A drain pipe dead-ends into the subfloor. Instead of draining outside of the house, it drains inside the house. Hah! Some fool plumber did that! Good thing we didn't call one. We might have gotten the same crook that installed this pipe."

I looked at my wife and my mother and all of the pieces of drywall and debris that now scattered that side of the house.

"Great," Lynn said.

"Yeah. Great," Mom said.

Despite their lack of enthusiasm and the reality of the disaster zone surrounding me, I savored another small win.

Now sitting in my favorite chair surrounded by chaos, I mentally prepared for the task at hand—removing the swimming pool from my living room.

"I'll call a plumber," Lynn said.

"No. Not this time," I said, standing up out of my chair. "I got this."

She gave me one of her looks. The look telling me that she knew I would say that and that she wanted to call a plumber because we both knew what would happen if I tried to fix the leak myself.

"A plumber will charge $75 just to show up and this whole house will be submerged by the time he gets here.

Then he'll charge us to fix something that I can do right now."

"Mel. Please, just call a plumber."

"I got it. I can do this. You'll see."

Some things a man must do himself. No matter how dumb that man is.

I went upstairs and saw that a valve to the sink had sprung loose. I knew exactly how to fix it because I had tightened the same valve three days earlier after noticing a small drip under the sink.

I raced to the garage to get my 5/8 inch socket wrench. I was prepared for this. I knew exactly where it was because just a few days ago I had reorganized my 376-piece socket set after it spilled its contents all over my garage floor.

I suspected that the crook that plumbed my house also made a living designing latches for toolboxes. It was the only explanation that made sense to me. You would expect someone who designs boxes for holding tools to know something about latches. Of course they do. They know just enough to design latches that trick one into thinking the lid is secure and shut. Then when one actually needs a tool, the latch fails so that the toolbox vomits tiny sockets and wrenches all over the floor.

I grabbed the lid and my toolbox exploded. After about twenty-seven minutes of rage and obscenities, I found the wrench. After thirty-two more minutes of rage and obscenities, I fixed the leak.

I stood there drenched in water and sweat and blood, observing the mangled ball of duct tape and hose clamps that surrounded the pipe. It was not pretty, but I had done it. I had stopped the leak and had done it long before any plumber could have arrived.

I heard the cheers from my children playing in the pond below me. I pretended the cheers were for me. It was another small victory in the never-ending war against my house. Standing in the doorway of the flooded bathroom, I raised my fists, closed my eyes, and yelled, "Take that, bitch!"

Looking back at the moment of celebration, I think I should have used a different phrase. It was not that I was above obscenities, so long as they were used well and at the proper occasion. It was more because when I opened my eyes, I was looking directly at my pregnant wife who happened to walk in right as I had unleashed my victory cry.

"Well," she said, "I still think we should have called a plumber."

She left as quickly as she came. I stood there too dumbstruck to utter another word. All went quiet, except I swear I heard my house snicker.

## CHAPTER 14

# *Charcoal*

J udd Nero and his dad sat in a dark bar on the out-
skirts of Savannah, waiting for Charcoal to arrive.
"You just do what I say and we'll be fine," Mori said.

"Sure, Mori," Judd said to his dad. "So what is all this about?"

"You'll find out."

"No. I'll find out right now. I left Sandy Pines and raced down the interstate with you without asking any questions. I deserve to know what this is about, otherwise, I'm going back."

"Fine."

"So what kind of drugs are you running this time?" Judd asked.

"I ain't running any drugs. And I ain't never run drugs."

"Sure."

"Besides, I spend too much time fishing down here to run drugs."

"Ok."

Mori leaned over and whispered, "Boy, don't you ever talk that way again. Not in the open. We're down here fishing. You understand!"

"Sure. Fishing. So what do you need me for? You've been down here fishing for years without me."

"Muscles."

"Muscles?"

"That's right. All those steroids you've been taking are going to come to use soon."

"I don't juice."

"Don't lie to me, boy. I know what you do. I've always known what you've been up to. I just never cared enough to do anything about it. Enough of that. I need you to lift lots of heavy fish because I'm planning on catching some big ones this year."

Judd leaned over and whispered, "I'm not in to catching your kind of fish. I got no problem with breaking the law. It's just too risky. It ain't worth it to me."

Mori whispered, "These fish are different. These are legal."

Judd sat back confused. Mori smiled. He took a drink, looked around, and leaned back over.

He whispered, "I ain't kidding either. These fish are legal. These fish are golden."

Mori winked at Judd and took another drink. Judd was even more confused now. It was rare that his dad attempted anything that involved following the law. Mori had made his living operating outside the law. The law was for suckers, Mori had always said. But Mori seemed serious and did not joke around about anything.

"What do you mean?" Judd asked.

Mori leaned over. "I was down here about a month ago. Right here in this bar. It's where I usually do business. I was waiting on a customer when this Charcoal fellow walks in. It was just us in the middle of the day. You'll know him when you see him. He's called Charcoal because that's exactly what he looks like, his skin all baked by the sun and jagged like the bark on one of those big oak trees. I was minding my business when he came over and sat next to me at the bar. Ordered up two beers without even asking. He gave me one and started talking. Just kept on talking and talking and I listened. It was annoying at first, until I realized that he was rich. Filthy rich."

Mori took another sip of his drink and then continued, "You would never know it looking at him with his ragged face and arms and hands. He talked about living in Key West on his boat with his wife and how he was traveling up the waterway to get a bigger boat and how he had made a fortune searching for treasure between Florida and South America. Anyway, I figured he was full of shit. But he was buying the beer, so I just let him go on."

"How do you know he's rich?"

"I'll tell you how I know. I was about to call bullshit on his story because I had enough of his beer and didn't want to hear him no more. Then this beautiful young woman comes walking into the bar. I mean she was drop-dead Hollywood gorgeous. She walks into this dump of a bar and straight to him. He said he had to go. And when he stood up, I noticed a gold coin hanging from a necklace he was wearing. You can imagine what I was thinking. I thought about running after him and introducing myself and offering help and all that nonsense, but my instincts kept me on that barstool."

Mori looked around to make sure no one was listening and then continued, "Paid off too. He showed up about thirty minutes later. He said his wife just needed some cash to go shopping. I could tell the fool was lonely and just wanted someone to listen to him talk about his treasure hunting. And I did listen. He talked about all the ships he had found and all the legal disputes between him and the other countries and about how he found them using old records of insurance claims and sonar and this and that. Then he stopped talking, leaned over like I'm doing right now and said, 'And we found one bigger than all of them put together.' That's what he said. Then he said, 'It is here in Georgia.'"

"No way," Judd said.

"That's what I thought. But he started talking about all the pirates who used to run these waters. Blackbeard included. He knew all about them and who they stole from and when and how much. 'It all came from old insurance records,' he said. He said he had found the mother lode. He found it using his sonar."

"I have never heard of it. That would have made the news."

"If the news knew about it. This Charcoal fellow may talk too much and may rightly be a fool, but he knows better than to announce his find until he knows he can keep it. That's his problem, you see. He tries to do things by the book. He wants to dive down and confirm the loot and then broker a deal with the government and the insurance companies before he tells them where it is."

"So what are we doing here?"

"Well, I had been listening to him go on and on and I had sized him up. I figured he was more lonely than anything, otherwise, why else would he be talking to me? I figured his beautiful wife was just about to drive him crazy, otherwise, he would have been with her. And I figured he was sizing me up too. That's when he asked me what I did. So I told him. I told him I was a fisherman and that I spent most of my time on these waters catching fish. I told him I didn't know nothing about making money or finding treasure, but that I knew these waters."

"A lie!"

"Of course it was a lie. But it was a lie he wanted to hear. Then I told him I have a son who's a good hand sometimes and strong."

"I see."

"And you can thank me for that later. Well, he took the bait. He said he needed help and he would share the loot with us if we could keep it a secret. Said he would split it fifty-fifty. Can you believe that? He said that wherever he found treasure, he made a local rich. He said it was both smart and good luck. He said that's how he got started and that he had enough money now anyway. He said it's easy to make money if you have money and that you can't take it with you."

Judd nodded in amazement.

Mori continued, "I pegged him for a fool when he first walked in. And I was right. I just didn't know he was a lucky fool. And we'll just go along with his foolish ways. But you listen here, I don't split nothing fifty-fifty. I know when I got the advantage on another man. And I'll have it. I just don't have it yet. He holds the cards right now. I did my homework before we came back down here. He's legit. I'm telling you, boy, you only get a chance like this once in a lifetime. Don't you screw it up."

It was all too wild to be true, but Judd knew his dad was too smart to chase such a thing unless it was for real. And it all sounded legal. He had never known his dad to work on anything unless it involved breaking the law. It must be for real.

On the other side of the bar, a door opened. In walked a man with a dark, ragged face with skin that looked like chunks of bark on a tree.

CHAPTER 15

# A Surprise

There was confusion as to exactly what happened at Tyler's birthday party, but one thing was clear—everyone blamed me.

Tyler was turning six, so we decided to throw a party and invite the neighborhood and some others. It would be a good opportunity to meet people in our community.

Both Lynn and I had found jobs near town, but I was still looking for work. Our original plan was for me to find a job that paid all our bills so Lynn could stay home with Tyler and Sophia and get ready for baby number three. As it worked out, we had to find two jobs, which still did not pay all our bills. I had thought that my experience in the military would transfer well to the civilian world.

"What do you think I am best suited for?" I asked a local recruiter.

She reviewed my résumé and past experience and then said, "You have an excellent résumé. You have a college degree, which is pretty much worthless these days, but it's there. What really stands out is your experience as an officer in the military. It's great leadership experience."

"So you are thinking about putting me in for high-level executive positions?" I asked.

"Oh no. Middle management for a large corporation is a much better fit," she said.

"What! I joined the military so I did not have to take that kind of job. I'll do anything but that. There must be something else. What about lower-level positions, like foreman or hourly laborer?"

"They make great money, especially with overtime," she said.

"Let's do that."

"No, that will not work."

"Why not?"

"You are overqualified."

"I don't understand."

"That means that you are overqualified on paper and underqualified in reality. They will never hire you."

"Oh," I said.

"Trust me. Look, what did you do in the military?" she asked.

"I was a leader."

"Ok. But what did you do, as in, what were your days and weeks like?"

"Well, generally, my boss would start the week telling me what he wanted done and then I would tell my people to do what my boss wanted done. At the end of the week, or sometimes at the end of the day depending on the boss, I would update my boss on the status of the work. There was a lot of reporting and a lot of meetings. In between filling out reports and attending meetings, I would listen to my people complain. They complained a lot. I would report these complaints to my boss. Then he would tell me to take care of it and to make sure my people got the job done. This went on for about eight years. Then I got out."

"See. That's perfect. You are a sure hire for middle management," she said.

"What is the pay?"

"Not good."

"So why should I take that kind of job?"

"You don't have any other options."

"Ok. I'll do it," I said.

I did not give up on hope. I thought that something better would present itself as I met more and more people in our community. None of my neighbors, however, helped much, or really at all, in my search for steady, high-paying employment. Most of them fit into one of three categories: they were retired, they were self-employed, or they were anarchists. My closest friend was my neighbor Otis. He was a great guy, but at eighty-five years of age and comfortably retired, he had different priorities.

Nor did my neighbors help with raising kids, primarily because our neighbors did not have any kids. So we invited all the kids in Tyler's class at school. I figured that about half of them would show up.

"They are all going to show up," Lynn said.

"What? That's ridiculous. They aren't going to drive way out here."

"They are going to show up. And so are their parents, probably both parents."

"What? That's crazy. I figured the parents would just drop off their kids and then come pick them up, you know, like normal people."

"Normal people don't do that anymore. Adults come to birthday parties to get to know the kid's parents," Lynn informed me. "They want to know if they can feel comfortable letting their children come over for play dates."

"Play dates? What are those?" I asked.

"That's what it is called when children get together."

"Whatever happened to just letting your children go outside and be home by dinner?"

"Parents don't do that anymore," she said. "It's considered unsafe, risky, and child neglect."

"Really!" I said. "My parents did it all the time. I remember clearly my mom making us go outside and then locking the door behind us."

"Ok. And how many times did you go to the emergency room before the age of five?"

"That's not important. The point is that parents these days worry too much. It can't be good for kids. Let's give the free-range approach a try."

"Free range?" she asked, putting her hands on her hips.

"You know, like eggs at the grocery store. What if you had to choose between a dozen eggs from chickens that were fed antibiotics and kept inside all day and a dozen eggs from chickens that were allowed to roam outside and eat natural foods, like bugs and corn and sawdust? You would, of course, pick the free-range eggs. Not the eggs from systematically engineered lumps of feathers we pass off as chickens. Chickens need freedom. Our children need freedom. Otherwise, they will grow up to be unprepared and weak without any clue as to how to live off the land. It will result in the wimpification of our children and eventually our entire society."

"What are you talking about? Is this one of your dumb ideas about getting out of work?"

"No. I'm talking about embracing a proven approach to life, that if followed can be applied to anything, including Tyler's party."

"You're talking nonsense. All I hear is you don't want to do anything. That's fine. What I need from you is to not try any of your tricks."

"Which tricks? You mean fun stuff like shooting off fireworks?"

"No fireworks."

"Can I make fart noises?"

"No."

"Come on. Kids love that stuff. There's nothing funnier than a well-timed fart, except maybe a surprise one."

"No!"

"Ok. Ok."

"It's really important that we make a good impression. Please, don't do anything stupid. Better yet, don't do anything. My mother has worked very hard to make this party a success. Everything is taken care of."

"All right. I'll try. I just want the kids to have a good time."

"My mom designed games just for this party. She has spreadsheets and checklists for each game. She created a program for the party, identifying the exact time and station where each game will be played. You don't have to worry about that."

That was my concern. My mother-in-law was an excellent planner. She planned everything. Everything for every day. And she expected her plans to be executed exactly as she had intended. That was my father-in-law's job.

My concern was that her games were not fun. They were too well organized and too well planned. I believed kids needed a certain amount of freedom to explore their own creativity. But so be it. One of the great by-products of not having to do anything for a party was that I did not have to do anything for the party. This gave me ample time to come up with something truly unique and fun.

Lynn's mom, Ms. Susie, proved to be an excellent planner and was very much a professional. Three months before the party, they chose a theme—pirates. Then they persuaded Tyler that he really wanted a pirate-themed party. During the next month of preparations, they made checklists. During the final month of preparations, they checked off their checklists. It all seemed too orderly for me.

Lynn and her mother had acquired pirate hats, pirate eye patches, inflatable pirate swords, and various pirate decorations. They even made little bags of pirate treasure to hand out as party favors. Pirate-themed programs detailed the day's events.

They prepared the party site—our house—with an artistic touch that would rival the finest of royal weddings. They decorated boxes as treasure chests. Even the trash cans were decorated with pirate-themed gems and treasure.

And Ms. Susie made a spectacular map.

"That treasure map is amazing," I said. "I have never seen such fine detail. And our yard is drawn perfectly to scale. The kids are going to love it."

"Treasure map? Oh, this. This is a layout showing where the tables and chairs go. I made this so you would know where to place everything."

"Oh, well. Thank you."

Ms. Susie had planned every detail. Still, I thought something was missing. I dared not make this thought known, especially during the final moments of preparation. Then it hit me. There were no surprises built into the party.

By planning and scripting every last detail, Lynn and her mom had forgotten to build in any surprises.

So far, I had done little to help. But I was now overwhelmed with a sense of duty that I needed to do something. Lynn and her mom were simply too focused on final preparations to entertain new ideas. In a little time, two visions of fun formed in my mind. One was simple and easy.

Fireworks. I had several large artillery-shell type fireworks that shot high into the air and burst into a big ball of brilliant colors. I could launch these at the end of the party, so technically this would not interfere with the party's schedule. A perfect end to a perfect party, I thought.

The second vision was even better. It struck me while I was in our shed looking at a spike buck I had mounted as a child. I was quite proud of the creature and thought it to be a fine work of art, especially for a young boy. For whatever reason, Lynn would not allow it in the house.

She said it looked like I had found it in the middle of a busy interstate. She also said it scared her.

I told her, "It looks just like a deer in the woods."

"I didn't know deer hissed at each other," she said.

"That shows you how much you know about deer! They don't hiss."

"Whatever. Just keep it where people can't see it."

"Fine, I'll put it in the shed."

The shed was my place. It was also the only place I could store my deer head, my fishing gear, my hunting gear, my camping gear, and in general it served as a museum of the past forty years of my life.

So far, I had kept up my end of the bargain, keeping the deer head in my shed. But Tyler's birthday called for an exception. It was time for the deer head to make an appearance and star in a little hunting game that my mind was in the process of inventing.

Danny and Wendy Ann arrived early. Danny found me working in my shed.

"Hey, man. Why are you taping ketchup packets to that mountain lion?" Danny asked.

"This here is a spike buck. Mounted it myself."

"No kidding. You did that yourself? Oh yeah, I see the two horns now."

"Yep, when I was a kid. Kept it all these years. It's a surprise for Tyler."

"You're giving him a deer head for his birthday?" he asked, taking a sip of his drink. He paused and thought about it for a few seconds while I worked away at the deer. "Cool."

"No. I'm not giving him my deer head. I'm making a deer hunting game. I'm going to put this spike buck in the hedges and let the kids shoot at it with a BB gun. After they hit some of the ketchup packets, I'll drag the deer off into the woods. Then they can practice following the blood trail until they find it, you know, just like a regular hunt."

Danny just stared at me.

"What did Lynn say about this?" he asked.

"I have not told her yet. I want to get it ready first. Why? Do you think she will like it?"

"I think she'll say the same thing I would."

"What's that?"

"Awesome!"

"You really think so?"

"Of course. Do you need any more ketchup?"

"Yes. Thank you. It's in the kitchen."

"You know," Danny said, returning with a handful of ketchup packets, "I think this deer game would be even better if it were a surprise for Lynn too."

"I don't know about that. I was going to run it by her first. You know she likes to have everything planned out."

"Yeah, but she's got so much to do. And it seems that everything is already planned out. This would just be a distraction at the last minute," Danny said.

"You might be right."

"And besides, we both know the kids will love it. It's a great idea," Danny said.

"Danny, you're right. I thought it was a great idea too. The kids need this. We'll just leave it in the shed right now."

I went to see how the other preparations were coming. Lynn asked me to go help Otis pick up the trash in his yard. Something had knocked his trashcan down and strewn garbage across his yard.

When I got there, he asked, "Did the coons get into your trash, too, last night?"

"No," I said.

"Tore mine to pieces and scattered it about the yard. Probably because I put fish bones in it."

Otis somehow always found time to fish, which I enjoyed because often he shared a cooler of fresh fish with me.

"I put my fish in the freezer," I said. "But that reminds me. I need to return the cooler you brought me yesterday. I set it out last night to air it out."

"Good idea," Otis said. "I used it as my bait cooler too. Probably stinks real bad. How is the birthday boy doing?"

"Good. You coming?"

"Yeah, I'll walk over."

I found Lynn and her mom and asked if there was anything I could do. They gave me the map and showed me where to put the tables and chairs. Soon, everything was in order.

Guests started arriving at 11:00.

"Wow. This is amazing," one mother said. "Who did all this?"

"That would be my mom," Lynn said.

"Oh, it was nothing," Ms. Susie said.

"And this cake. I have never seen anything like it. Where did you buy it?"

"My mom made that too."

"Unbelievable."

I later learned that there are birthday cakes that are not for eating. This was one of them. Ms. Susie also made smaller cakes that looked just like the large cake. The smaller cakes were for eating.

Guests streamed in for the first fifteen minutes, gushing over the beauty and perfection of each remarkable detail. Ms. Susie allowed this to carry on for exactly fifteen minutes. Then the games commenced.

Children were pulled from trees and fences and then corralled over to station one. It involved some stacked cups and water guns. The kids loved it and so did Ms. Susie. The party progressed perfectly and according to the schedule.

After the children began playing games, Dr. Manning arrived.

"Hello, Dr. Manning!" I said as he walked down our driveway. "Thanks for stopping by."

"Thank you for the invite. This is my first time out here. It is so very peaceful."

"Most of the time, unless you have a bunch of children running around in your yard."

He looked toward the backyard, where the children were engaged in one of Ms. Susie's games.

"It seems to me they are all quite well behaved. What are they doing back there, playing some sort of marching game?"

"I don't know. I'm trying to stay out of it. Anyway, can I get you a drink or something to eat?"

"Yes. Please."

"A beer?"

"No, thank you. Just water if you have it."

"Sure. Come over here, I want to introduce you to some of my family."

"Is your father here?"

"No. Not right now, but he'll be here later. You should stay for awhile after the party."

"I think I might, thank you," he said.

We walked over to where Danny and a group of other men stood.

"Danny, this is Dr. Manning," I said. "He's the one who treated me after I got attacked by the no-see-ums."

"Hi, doc, nice to meet you," Danny said.

"And you as well."

"I told him to wear long pants and a long shirt," Danny said.

"Yes, that would have been preferable."

"I guess he might listen to his brother-in-law next time."

"Enough, Danny," I said.

"Mel and I go way back. See, growing up we were good friends. Then I married his sister."

"Danny. Enough."

"Can you believe that! Anyway, I have always tried to help Mel, but he just doesn't listen."

· "Danny!"

Fortunately, Danny became distracted by a man walking down the middle of the road mumbling to himself. The man was dressed in rags, all held together by a rope at his waist. He wore old sandals and had a ragged beard that hung down past his chest. It was Pastor David. He had been this way for about a month.

"Who invited Jesus?" Danny said.

"That's Pastor David," I said. "He's a neighbor and on hard times right now."

"What happened?" Danny asked.

"No one knows. Until a few months ago, he had a perfectly clean house, a perfectly cut yard, and he didn't drink."

"Strange."

"Yeah, all the other neighbors thought so too," I said. "They said it was just a matter of time before he flipped. Anyway, he flipped. It happened on Easter at church. He zoned out in the middle of the service and has been this way since."

"Here he comes. What's in the plastic cup?" Danny asked.

"I don't know, but it smells like gasoline," I said.

"He seems a little different," Danny said.

"My mother often told me to be very nice to people who are different," I said.

"Good policy," Dr. Manning said.

"Especially if they are your neighbors," Danny said.

Pastor David walked over to our group of men.

"Hello, Pastor David," I said. "How are you today?"

"Huh. Oh. Yes. I am, thank you," he said.

"Good to hear. Please join us," I said.

We continued talking in our group until it was time for the children to eat.

"We are about to eat," Ms. Susie announced. "Everyone to the porch, please."

We followed our instructions and proceeded to the porch.

"Would anyone like to lead us in prayer?" Ms. Susie asked.

Silence.

"Anyone?" she asked.

"Pastor David," I said. "Could you please say a prayer for us?"

"Huh? What waz that? Prayer. Oh. No, thank you. I'm trying to quit," he said, darting his eyes about while taking another sip from his plastic cup.

"Alrighty then," I said. "I'll do it. Let us bow our heads. Dear Lord, thank you for this food and our time together. Please bless all those who are less fortunate than us. Amen."

The children began eating while the adults continued to mingle. I walked to the house to get a couple of beers. Right before I opened the door, I saw Ms. Susie carrying two chairs to my shed.

Oh no, I thought. She'll see the surprise.

I ran in hope I could beat her there.

I heard a loud scream in the shed, "Ahhh! Shoo cat! Shoo! Get! Get! Awaaayy!"

Then I heard crashing and clashing in the shed. When I arrived, I found Ms. Susie on the ground breathing hard and trying to push the deer off her. Lynn arrived soon after me. I was tending to the mess.

"Oh no!" Lynn said. "There's blood everywhere. Mom, did you break anything?"

"Yes," I said. "Just snapped in two like a chicken bone."

"Oh dear. I'll call an ambulance."

"An ambulance? That won't help. We can just glue it back after the party. It will set after a day or so and then we can sand it until it looks like fresh bone."

"What! Just leave her there. I'll go get Dr. Manning."

"He doesn't need to get involved. I can take care of it." I showed Lynn the broken antler and explained that her mom had crashed into the game I invented.

Lynn just stared at me.

"I wanted it to be a surprise."

Blank stare.

"You know, a surprise game for the kids."

Blank. Stare. Of death.

I helped wipe the ketchup off Ms. Susie and then showed them what was left of my game and explained with great enthusiasm how I had planned to surprise everyone with a deer hunting station.

"And if they hit the deer just right," I said, "the ketchup packets would explode! Then I would drag the deer head through the yard and into the woods as if it ran away wounded. Then the kids could track the deer together, looking for fake blood in the yard!"

My mother-in-law sat there in silence, her mouth open. Lynn was shaking her head.

"How do you come up with this stuff?" Lynn asked.

"Easy. You just have to think like a six-year-old."

"That explains a lot."

"Thank you."

Lynn and her mother went back to the party, which continued to progress as planned despite Ms. Susie's fall.

My hunting game was ruined, but at least I still had the giant fireworks.

The party continued without a blemish and in general turned out to be a great event. Ms. Susie's creativity amazed all the guests, from the toddlers to the adults. The kids loved every part of the party. It was clear the party had achieved the perfection that Lynn and her mom had expected.

Toward the end of the party, the flock of happy children moved to the middle of station four. Squeals of joy echoed across the yard. I could tell Lynn was very pleased. She moved from guest to guest, thanking them for coming.

I was in the middle of a conversation with Dr. Manning and the other men when I remembered the fireworks.

"Sorry, guys, I almost forgot," I said, running toward the shed.

"Forgot what?" Dr. Manning asked. "Do you need help?"

"No. It's a big surprise for the kids."

I passed Ms. Susie as she was leading kids through the station.

I winked at her and said, "Watch this."

Lynn saw me running and went over to Dr. Manning and asked, "Why was Mel running toward the shed?"

"I don't know. He said something about a big surprise."

"Oh no."

As I was opening the door to the shed to get the fireworks, I noticed the stinky cooler still sitting in my driveway.

Odd. It was closed shut. The fish smell must have been cooking in it all day. I needed to move it before someone else discovered it. The cooler had a triangular-shaped top that locked automatically when swiveled into place. Hmm, I thought. I guess I better open it back up to let it air out.

I tried to open the cooler but it was jammed. I pulled harder.

Boom! The top came off and a raccoon sprung out as if its ass were on fire. With claws and fangs stretched, he landed on me. We wrestled and fought and flailed in the driveway, both trying to figure out what in the hell had just happened.

The raccoon broke free and bolted off, straight toward the flock of happy children.

In vain, I raced after it.

"Oh my God!" one mom yelled.

"What the hell!" said one of the men.

"Puppy dog!" a toddler said.

The flock of children screamed a giant scream that radiated out like a human firecracker with frightened kids popping off in every direction.

In the center of the chaos and madness stood Ms. Susie, unmoved and staring at me and at the raccoon racing directly toward her.

I tripped on one of the children. The speed of the encounter launched my body into an uncontrolled spiral toward Ms. Susie. It was then that I learned that raccoons can and do fly. Seeing me tumbling through the air frightened the coon into an eight-foot leap over Ms. Susie's head and onto the large birthday cake. I, on the other hand, rolled until I stopped at her feet.

Brushing the dirt and blood off, I stood up to face the stunned crowd of moms and dads.

"Uhhh, surprise," I said.

Silence.

Pastor David mumbled, "Crazy-ass neighbor."

For whatever reason, the parents took these signs as their cue to go home.

Trying to salvage what was left of the perfect party, Ms. Susie went from kid to kid, making sure they left with their small bags of pirate treasure.

Tyler and a few of the boys circled the house in search of the raccoon.

After the party, while Lynn and others were cleaning up, I found a few minutes to sit in my chair in the living room. I was exhausted. Reflecting on the day's events, I wondered how such a terrible thing could happen. After a few more minutes, I decided that such a thing could not have happened and in fact did not happen. This brought me peace.

I put my legs up on a small cloth-covered table, relaxed, and pretended that all was well. Then the table started giggling at me.

"What's going on in here!" I said.

A child crawled out and into my lap.

"Hey, kid," I said, giving Tyler a big hug and frazzling his hair.

"Did you have a good birthday?" I asked.

"Yes," he said with a big smile. "It was the best."

"Yeah? What was so great about your birthday?"

"I liked it when you chased that little dog across the yard."

I held him close and read a book until we both started nodding off.

Then I heard a little girl laugh. It wasn't Sophia, but I recognized the voice.

"Who's there?" I asked.

I searched the room but found no one.

CHAPTER 16

## Good for Nothing

Lynn and her mother were busy cleaning up the kitchen after the party.

"Someone left her child behind!" I said.

"Who? Where?" Lynn asked.

"I don't know, but I heard a little girl laughing in our living room."

"Did you see her?"

"No. I was dozing off when I heard her."

"Oh. I see. You were sleeping while we were busy cleaning and you think you heard someone's child."

"I swear I heard a child laughing and I'm pretty sure she was laughing at me. She must have run off and hid again."

Lynn's mother stopped cleaning dishes for a moment.

"I'll help find her," Ms. Susie said.

"I'll look too," Lynn said. "But I think you are hearing things. Go see if your guests saw anything."

"Guests?"

"That's right, your guests. Danny has been hosting Dr. Manning and Pastor David while you were napping."

"That's right," I said. "I asked Dr. Manning to stay."

I ran outside to the group of men.

"Hey, guys. Did you happen to see or hear a little girl recently?" I asked. "I think one of the parents left their child here."

"No. I thought everyone had left about an hour ago," Dr. Manning said.

"I heard a child in my living room and I think she ran off somewhere else. Danny, can you help me find her?"

"No need," Danny said.

"What do you mean, no need? A parent could have left their child here."

"Nope. Didn't happen," he said.

"How do you know?"

"I'm telling you. No parent left their child at your house."

"I don't know, I heard something. We should at least look."

"I'm telling you, Mel. It's a waste of time. We're better off doing nothing."

"I swear, Danny. You are and always have been the laziest person I know. It is an absolute miracle that you are not broke and living under a bridge."

"Waz that? Somebody call me?" Pastor David asked.

"Easy, man," Danny said. "I'm doing all right."

"All right! You live in a huge mansion on the water with enough money to waste on paying others to cut your grass and clean your house and deliver food and do anything else you want. And you act like it's nothing!"

"Really?" Dr. Manning asked. "How did you build your wealth so quickly?"

"It was nothing," Danny said.

"See!" I said.

"No. Really," Danny said. "It was nothing. That's the secret."

"I do not understand," Dr. Manning said.

"A lot of people get rich by doing nothing. Some are just better at it than others. I happen to be one of those. I think it's more instinct than anything else. Like Mel said, I've always been good at doing nothing." Danny said, taking a sip of his drink.

"Let me explain," Danny continued. "When I moved here, what do you think I had?"

"Nothing."

"Right. So what did I have to lose?"

"Nothing."

"Exactly. So I had complete freedom to do anything. Or nothing. From what I could tell, there were a lot of people around me busting it at school or whatever. It seemed to me they were just getting into more and more debt."

"That's my story," Dr. Manning said. "I had half a million in debt before I finished my degrees. And it took me nine years to build that debt."

"Right," Danny said. "So while you and Mel and the rest of the world were taking out loans and mortgages and credit card debt, I did nothing. Without doing anything, I was half a million dollars and nine years ahead of you."

"For sure," Dr. Manning said. "I would have given almost anything to come out of medical school debt free. I spent the next four years in residency, working every day for what seemed to be less than nothing."

"Yep," Danny said. "Well, during my first six months here, I sold cars."

"That sounds like something," I said.

"Not really. I heard about the gig from a friend one morning. He said anyone could work at the car dealership. No hourly requirements. The salary was nothing, all commissions. But what got my attention was the free breakfast. He said the dealership had donuts and coffee and boiled eggs for all the salesmen. What do I have to lose? I figured. I'll just go work at the dealership and get a free breakfast out of it."

"Sounds like you," I said.

"Anyway. I showed up and ate my free breakfast. And my friend was right. There were no requirements to do anything. But I learned quickly that car salesmen work hard."

"So, you didn't last?" I said.

"No. The opposite. I just sat back and ate breakfast and drank coffee while the other salesmen swarmed about the lot, looking, almost begging, for someone to buy a car. It was pitiful. There was this one salesman, an older fellow, he had been in the business for over fifty years, doing nothing else but selling cars. He had stage IV lung cancer. And he showed up every morning. Can you believe that?  It was amazing to watch that old man work."

"Wow," Dr. Manning said.

"What was even more amazing," Danny said, "was that he had been fighting stage IV lung cancer for over forty of the fifty years he had been selling cars. Of course, he was such a humble old man that he never let his customers know he had been fighting it that long. Anyway, he was the lead salesman. Held all the records."

"Impossible," Dr. Manning said.

"Terrible," I said.

"I blew all of his records away in the first six months," Danny said.

"No way. How? What did you do?" I asked.

"Nothing. I simply sat back and watched the show. Soon customers got tired of getting hassled by the swarm of salesmen. They would come over to the breakfast table and ask me about the cars. I told them I did not know a thing about cars, but they could take one for a ride. Keep it for the day, if they wanted to. Well, the manager found out about this and man did he get mad. Tried to fire me on the spot. I told him that was fine and that I would leave, but there were no hard feelings. Before he could fill out the paperwork, I had sold ten cars. In less than a day. No one had ever done that."

"Amazing," Dr. Manning said. "It makes sense to me."

"I kept this up for months and cars flew off the lot. Some of the other salesmen tried my approach, but they couldn't do it. I don't think they were capable of doing it."

"Of what?" I asked.

"Of doing nothing. They tried, but it came off insincere. Most of them lived to hassle someone. They couldn't do it any other way. That old man who had been dying of cancer finally recovered from his cancer and then retired. He said he just couldn't get motivated anymore now that his cancer had gone away. I made a fortune, but this made all the other salesmen furious. So they decided to buy me out."

"Buy you out of what?" I asked.

"Nothing. I did not own a stake or anything in the dealership. They just got together and agreed to pay me a percent of their sales as long as I quit. Well, I had made enough already to retire without that deal. But I took it and I bought my house with cash and left that place. I get checks every month. For doing nothing."

"Wild," Dr. Manning said.

"Yeah. Wendy Ann thinks so too. She's the hardest working person I know. Still is, despite all of our money. Anyway, she is not offended by my success because she knows that, under the surface, I'm really not that good at anything."

"Except nothing," Dr. Manning said.

"Exactly. I didn't stop with selling cars. I had met so many people and they now trusted me so I got into real estate. Now that's a gig. I truly do nothing and get paid three percent."

"Three percent?" I asked.

"Yep. People come to me and say they want to sell their house. I say fine and I put it on a list, the MLS."

"MLS?" I asked.

"Multiple Listing Service. It's the biggest racket I know. And legal, too, if not required. I put it on the MLS and someone else sells it. Realtors are worse than car salesmen when it comes to hassling customers. They run around all day trying to sell houses. They don't care if their customer is buying or selling. Well, once the house is sold, I get three percent. All I did was put it on a list."

Dr. Manning shook his head. "With my student loans and mortgage, I'm now over one million dollars in debt. I do not even want to look at college tuition for my children."

"You should look into selling makeup," Danny said. "I can get you into it. It's nothing."

"You gotta be kidding me," I said. "I never knew you sold makeup."

"I haven't. I've never sold a single item, but I make millions off of it."

"How?" I asked.

"I'm not exactly sure how it works. There's some crazy math involved, but I know one thing—it adds up to a crazy amount of money. It all started when a lady asked me to sell her house. So I listed it and it sold within days. She came back and thanked me even though I never did a thing. She said that she knew a good salesperson when she saw one and asked if I wanted to sell makeup. And of course I told her no. Then she said that I did not have to actually sell makeup or do anything unless I wanted to. Now I was interested. Then she started talking about some magic penny.

She said that if a penny doubled every day for thirty days, that the penny would be worth millions of dollars, in just thirty days. Can you believe that?"

"No," Dr. Manning said.

"Yes," I said.

"Humph," Pastor David grunted.

"And it would keep growing to hundreds of millions," Danny said. "Well, I did not care too much about the money, but my instinct said to go for it, which was easy considering all I had to do was nothing. See, she said that I would be assigned a referral code and that everyone who signed up because they learned about the job from me would fall under my referral code. I would get a percentage of their sales. And if they referred anyone else, I would get a percentage of their sales. And so on. And so on. It was like a giant make-believe money tree, except for real. I referred a couple of go-getters and all of a sudden I'm making millions again. Off makeup. What do you think about that?"

"Smart," Dr. Manning said. "By the time I make any money, I'll be old and have no use for it."

"He's just lucky," I said.

"God-damned genius," Pastor David said.

"That's pretty much it as far as money goes. But it works for other things too," Danny said.

"Like what?" I asked.

"Folding laundry. I don't know why people fold laundry. It's such a waste of time. Just buy another dryer and take the clothes right out of the dryer."

"Yeah?" Dr. Manning said.

"Putting up dishes. Again, wasteful. Just have two dishwashers. Don't even need cabinets."

Danny took another sip of his drink and then continued, "Cutting grass. It's just going to go dormant every winter anyway. Just let it go, unless you want to donate your money to someone who will cut it for you. I could go on and on but I think you get it now. Most of the time it's better to do nothing, you'll end up in the same place either way."

"It's like treating a cold," Dr. Manning said.

"Or cleaning up after kids," I said.

"Life," Pastor David said.

Lynn and her mother joined us.

"What are you guys talking about?" she asked.

"Nothing," I said.

"Well, while you have been standing around talking about nothing, we looked all over the house and yard for some parent's missing child."

"I'm out," Pastor David said.

"I think I'll be going now," Dr. Manning said. "Thank you for inviting me. It was a great party."

"Thank you for coming," Lynn said. "It was a great party and I have my mom to thank for that. I'm so sorry that it ended the way it did and that my husband is an idiot."

"No. No," Dr. Manning said. "I found it all quite entertaining. I would love to come back anytime you ask."

After Dr. Manning and Pastor David left, Lynn continued, "For the past thirty minutes, we have been chasing your imagination all over this house and found nothing. There is no one else here."

"That's a relief," I said.

"See," Danny said. "All is well that ends well."

"Next time," Lynn said. "Before you send us on a manhunt, you should think about . . . what is that in our yard?"

"What?" I asked.

"That."

"That is Dad's truck," I said. "He must have just arrived."

"I know that is your dad's truck. What is that attached to his truck? Did you have anything to do with this?" Lynn asked.

"Nothing. I promise," I said.

I did my best to stay calm and cool and control my emotions and pretend that it was all about nothing, but that was hard to do while sprinting toward a white work of art gracefully gleaming on a trailer in my backyard.

CHAPTER 17

## *There Is Treasure Out There*

Her beautiful, perfect curves were simply irresistible. It was as if she were softly calling my name, saying touch me and I'll be yours. Drawn toward her by some powerful magnetism, I walked over to her. Unable to resist the urge, I extended my hand and caressed her beautiful curves as she sparkled in the sunlight.

"What do you think, Son?" Dad asked.

"She's beautiful," I said.

"This is disgusting," Lynn said.

"I had not planned on bringing her home. But as soon as I saw her all alone in the parking lot, I knew I had to have her. If I didn't, someone else would."

"What is wrong with you men? Does your brain just shut down every time you look at a boat?" Lynn said.

"How did you find her?" I asked.

"Luck and destiny, I guess," Dad said.

"Tyler. Don't pay any attention to this," Lynn said. "Your father and your grandfather are not behaving. Let this be a lesson to you—grown men should not act this way."

"Just let it go, dear," Lynn's mother said. "There's nothing you can do about it. They are just wired this way. Some things will never change."

"Dad, I can't believe you bought me a boat," I said.

"Good," he said, "because I didn't."

"Well, that's a relief," Lynn said. "Maybe there is hope for mankind."

"Did you rent it for the day?" Lynn's mother asked.

"No," Dad said. "Nobody rents boats. That's like renting a dog or something. I bought it for me."

"Oh," I said.

"Oh no," Lynn said.

"But you know, I figured I could maybe leave it down here for awhile. I mean, Mel lives closer to the water and all. It'll save me time trailering it," he said, giving me one of his winks.

Brilliant, I thought.

"Fools," Lynn said. "You men will never learn."

"Huh?" I said.

"What?" Dad said.

"In what world and under what reasoning do you think having a boat at this time in our lives is a good idea? It is just going to cost us a bunch of money that we don't have."

"Huhhh . . ." I responded.

Dad searched the hull for nicks and scratches.

"Look," Lynn said. "I'm exhausted. I'm tired of cleaning and chasing children, both real and imaginary. And there is still a lot more to do. I don't have time for this right now. Come on, Mom, let's go back inside while these men ogle over this, this thing. Neither one of them will ever listen."

And they left.

"What did she say?" Dad asked.

"I don't know. I wasn't paying attention," I said. "I think she just wants a little time alone right now."

"Probably. Women sometimes act strangely around boats. They're just wired that way," Dad said.

"Kids!" I said to Tyler and Sophia, "go inside and tell your mom that Dad and I are going fishing."

"Can we go with you?" Tyler asked.

"No."

"Please!" Tyler pleaded.

"No. It's better that you stay here with your mom, especially considering the mood she's in right now. Just tell her I'm going fishing."

I sent the kids in to tell Lynn we were leaving. Before Dad and I could get out of the driveway, Tyler and Sophia came running toward us with life jackets on.

"Mom said we could go with you!" Tyler said.

Hmm, I thought, maybe she likes the boat after all.

Dad and I drove to the marina. It was Saturday and there was a long line of trucks waiting to launch their boats.

"She's only about fifteen feet, but that's good," Dad said. "It means you don't have to carry all the emergency equipment required on sixteen footers and larger."

"Smart," I said.

"Yeah. Keeping up with radios and flares and other useless gear can be a real hassle when you're trying to get on the water. That stuff expires too. We'll save some money by keeping it simple."

"Real smart."

"Scott men have been known to make bad decisions, you know that, right?"

"I know."

"I am trying to change that," he said.

"Yeah, I wish I were better at making good decisions. I think some people are just luckier than others. Take Danny, for instance, he was always the laziest person around. Never did well in school. Always did just enough."

"Yeah, I know," Dad said. "He drove me nuts when y'all were growing up."

"Look at him now," I said. "Still lazy and dumb, but filthy rich."

"Yeah. Some people are just lucky. That's all he's got going for him."

"That and being married to your daughter."

"Thanks for reminding me."

"Look at that!" I said.

"Wow. She must be at least thirty feet with a nine-foot beam," Dad said.

"Tyler, look at that huge boat," I said. "Maybe we'll get there someday."

"Maybe," Dad said. "But this skiff of mine is a great starter boat. It'll get us on the water."

"Yeah, when the kids are bigger we'll need a bigger boat. I wonder how much it costs to put two engines on a boat."

"I don't know," Dad said. "We'll have to look into it in a few years. I'm not giving up hope on getting rich. We just need to keep our eyes open for the right opportunity. That's how you get rich, Son. The trick is being smart enough to see the opportunity when it presents itself."

"Daddy!" Tyler said. "Look at that one. It's just like ours!"

I turned to see the top half of a seventy-foot yacht docked at the marina.

"It's a little different," I said. "But I like your attitude, kid. We'll have to work up to one that big."

"No, Daddy. Not the big one. There's a little one on the back of the big one. It looks just like ours."

"It sure does," I said. "I like where you're going with this. There's no need to sell our little skiff. We'll just keep it so we have it to put on the back of a bigger boat someday."

"Will that save us some money?" Tyler asked.

"Yes, of course," I said.

The line of trucks and boats was long. I quickly tired of waiting, in part because of the wait but mostly because the air conditioning in my dad's truck did not work.

"Dad, can you take the kids to the tabby house and wait there? I think it's going to be a while."

"Sure. Come on, kids."

They left, but the trucks did not move. I kept the windows down to try and stay cool. The longer I waited, the more I felt we needed to hurry up and get on the water.

"Dad," I said, "I'll get the boat in as fast as I can. Y'all just meet me at the dock."

"Take your time, Son. There's no rush."

The more I sat still, the more I wanted to go.

"You going fishing?" asked a nearby voice.

Under one of the large oaks sat a man with rough, charred skin. He blended in with the trunk of the tree. The sun had taken its toll. He could have been seventy-five or thirty-five. It was impossible to tell. He sat there drinking cheap beer and seemed to be in no hurry.

"Maybe," I said, not really wanting to engage in conversation. I was still focused on getting my boat in the water. "Might try to catch a redfish."

"You catch many reds around here?" he asked.

"Not really. I mostly catch stingrays."

"I've caught my share of stingrays."

"Ever ate stingray?" I asked.

"Once," he said.

"Me too. It's not bad. But it's not good either."

"I like your boat."

"Thank you," I said. "It's easy to fish out of. I don't have to worry about getting stuck in the mud when I'm in the marsh grass."

The trucks ahead of me were still not moving.

"This place really is in the boonies, ain't it?" the man said.

"Yes," I said. "But some people like it that way."

"Not my wife. She wanted to go all the way to Savannah. But we were almost out of gas. I saw a sign for a marina. It was a godsend. I couldn't believe there was a marina way out here."

"Where are you coming from?"

"Key West."

The trucks ahead of me looked like they were about to move. Good, I thought. I was ready to get on the water.

"Key West, you say," I said. "I love Key West. It's one of my favorite places."

"Too many people now," he said. "I've been down there for work for years. We're moving up the coast now."

"What were you doing in Key West?"

He looked at me, put down his beer, and opened another one.

"Treasure hunting," he said.

That was a first. If he asked, I guess I could be an astronaut.

"What brings you up here?" I asked.

"I just got a new boat," he said. "My other one was too small."

"Yeah. What kind of boat is it?"

Then he pointed to the seventy-footer docked at the marina.

"Well," I said, "it's kind of hard to fish the marsh grass in that."

"True, but I go fishing with the one on the back."

I knew a little bit about treasure hunters—the real ones. I knew enough to know that the few treasure hunters who actually found sunken ships became embattled in complex legal disputes over who owned it. Usually foreign countries and old insurance companies kept most of the loot.

"I got another little boat," he said. "She's all black, my night rider. I keep her inside the big one."

"Yeah?"

"She's my lucky boat. She was with me when we found the *San José*," he said.

"I think I heard about that," I said.

"She sunk with over $500 million in gold and silver."

"Did you get any of that?"

"A lot of it."

"You must have had good lawyers."

"We had great lawyers."

"No kidding."

"We found a bunch of coins like this one," he said, lifting a necklace that ran through a single, large coin. It was marked with a spear piercing a heart.

"Pirate treasure," he said. "The smartest pirates melted the gold and made their own coins. We found another wreck."

"Where?" I asked.

"I can't say," he said. "That's a secret. I sure ain't telling the government where it is. But they know I found it. This time I'm negotiating my rights first."

"Good decision," I said.

"This one is worth over a billion," he said, taking another sip of his beer.

It would have been obvious to any reasonably intelligent and half-employed person to introduce himself to this stranger in hopes of the off chance he was telling the truth and needed help, with anything.

The trucks ahead started to move. Time to go.

"Interesting," I said. "Good luck with your boat and your treasure hunting. Tonight, you should go to The Wreck. It is a restaurant next to this marina. You should take your wife there for dinner. She'll enjoy it. My name is Mel and my neighbor runs it. Just tell them I sent you."

"Thank you. I'm Charlie, but everyone calls me Charcoal," he said, taking another sip of his beer. "I'll try, but my wife wants to get to Savannah. But thank you again and good luck with your fishing. Maybe I'll see you around."

I left Charcoal behind and unloaded Dad's boat as quick as I could.

I met Dad and the kids down at the floating dock. We got in the skiff and drove away. As I was driving away, I looked back and saw a woman get out of the yacht. She walked over to Charcoal. Like the yacht, she was sleek and beautiful and I could tell she was mad at Charcoal for stopping way out in the boonies.

Still focused on getting away from the marina and off into the marsh, I soon forgot about Charcoal and his treasure hunting. A few hours later, while we were fishing, all was still and calm. The marina was far behind us and out of sight.

"About five miles from here is Blackbeard Island," Dad said.

"Yeah?"

"I spent a lot of days there as a kid," he said.

"Blackbeard Island? You mean, like the pirate?" I asked.

"Yes. Long ago, pirates ruled this place, if such a place can be ruled. When I was growing up, the shrimpers were the pirates. They ran drugs because it was easy. There is still no law out here."

"Dad," I said, "you'll never believe what this guy just told me."

I told Dad every detail, from his appearance to his wife. From his yacht to his skiff. I told him about the gold coin, the *San José*, and everything else.

"Did you ask him if he needed any help?" Dad asked.

"No."

"Did you get his phone number or give him yours?"

"No."

"Son," Dad said, "did I ever tell you that Scott men have a history of making bad decisions?"

"Yes."

"We need to go back. Now."

"I see. You're right," I said. "Maybe he went to the restaurant. He might still be there when we get back."

"Maybe," Dad said.

We reeled in the lines and rushed back to the marina. Charcoal's yacht was gone.

CHAPTER 18

# *Evil*

Why are some children mean?
The Wreck had a tree house outside where children often played while the adults waited for the food to arrive. We were eating dinner at The Wreck when the question popped in my mind—Why are some children mean? Not just mean, but evil mean.

At the time, I was not sure why this thought came to my mind, but I knew exactly, to every last detail and every last freckle on his face, which childhood bully had prompted the question.

I felt his presence on the bluff. The sensation I experienced was much more than a premonition. It was something else, something supernatural, and fate later proved that to be true.

For no logical or rational reason, hate—raw hate—filled my mind and soul. I had not seen or heard from him in over twenty years, but I felt his presence as if he were standing right behind me.

Except for the tree house, I saw nothing and heard nothing that should have triggered his image. I had seen a thousand tree houses and a thousand bullies and none of these had ever brought back his memory. But what I sensed that evening was more than a bad memory. He was near me now, and somehow I knew it.

From The Wreck, I could see boats, mostly local fishing boats, coming back to the marina. One of the boats was Charcoal's yacht.

"Lynn, I need you to stay with the kids. I'm going over to the marina," I said.

"Ok. What is it?" she asked.

"I'll tell you later. Trust me. I need to go."

I drove next door to the marina and saw Charcoal on his yacht. There were two other men with him working on the deck. One was skinny and older. The other was a large man about my age, it seemed. Even from the back, he looked familiar and I wondered if I had seen him before. I started to get out of my truck and approach the yacht when the larger man turned and I saw his face. I recognized every last freckle.

My heart dropped. Judd Nero. Impossible. But it was him—Judd Nero. It could have been anyone else—the devil himself—but not Judd Nero. How did this happen! He should have been in Sandy Pines or in prison or dead or somewhere else where he belonged, not standing on my one opportunity in life to get rich.

My mind raced back to the first day of kindergarten in Sandy Pines, when I met Judd face-to-face. We had moved to the town during the middle of the school year. Dad had taken a job at a sawmill. We lived outside of Sandy Pines, near the sawmill.

The school was a mill-town school. There were good kids and bad kids there, just like any other school. Most were poor by any standard, but all kids are poor. At my school, fights often broke out.

Instead of being decorated with swing sets and seesaws and monkey bars, the playground was decorated with pine trees and dirt.

This all mattered little to us because we were allowed to roam free at recess and that was enough. There was little to no adult supervision. Like most children, we played tag and hide-and-seek and chase and all the other games kids play when they do not have toys.

Some of the kids found entertainment in simply walking around and watching other kids play. My new friend Sammy was one of these. He was perfectly content to watch others play. It also allowed him to get away quickly when the first-graders arrived.

I met Judd Nero on my first day at recess. He was in the first grade. For whatever reason, kindergarten recess and first-grade recess overlapped by about ten minutes. A first bell signaled the beginning of first-grade recess and a second bell signaled the end of kindergarten recess.

The first part of recess was quite pleasant. Sammy took me around and showed me all of his favorite pine trees and places where he dug for treasure and holes where small animals lived. It was clear that he enjoyed recess. Then the bell rang—the first bell—and Sammy's demeanor changed.

"Quick! Hide! The first-graders are coming," Sammy said running toward the trees.

"What? Ok," I said, slowly following him.

"Let's go! To the trees," Sammy said.

"All right, I guess."

We were standing behind one of the larger pines when Sammy said, "That's Nero."

He pointed to the large kid being followed by a group of smaller kids. Like a pack of hungry wolves, they marched toward the trees.

"Stay behind the tree. Whatever you do, stay behind the tree," Sammy said. "There is a chance he will not see us."

Even at the age of five, it all seemed dumb to me. I left Sammy standing behind the tree and walked directly toward Nero.

One might think I did this because I was large and un-afraid. The reality was that I was small—tiny, in fact—and clueless. Even when compared to small kids, I seemed small. I remained this way through most of high school until I hit a growth spurt. My dad was six-foot-four and a giant of a man, so in my mind I too was a giant. And my parents never told me otherwise.

Throughout middle school, other parents would comment to my parents or to no one in particular, "Mel is so tiny. He should not even be out there on that football field. He is going to get injured."

And they were right. The coach had to special order pants because the extra smalls fell down on me. And I did get injured, often, because I did not know I was supposed to back down from larger, stronger players.

So when people told me I was too small for this or that, I did not believe them. I had something else going for me, something more powerful than confidence—I had igno-rance.

"Mel, come back!" Sammy said.

I just kept walking toward Nero with no real purpose or plan, except that my mind and body felt compelled to con-front him in an almost involuntary way. In almost no time, he saw me and we met in the middle of the playground.

Within seconds, the kids on that playground had formed a circle around Nero and me.

I approached Nero with the confidence of someone who had never been beaten up. This was because I had never been beaten up, but only because I had never been in a fight. I had never had a reason to fight. I was only in kindergarten!

Even back then, Nero stood taller and broader than everyone around him. His size alone should have caused me to back down.

Then the chants began.

"Fight!"

"Fight!"

"Fight!"

The circle grew larger and the chants grew louder. Almost every breathing soul on that dirt field yearned for a fight. And there I stood in the middle of that human ring on my first day of school in a new town about to get my ass kicked.

"Fight!"

"Fight!"

"Fight!"

Nero looked at me and circled. Slowly. He circled. He stared at me and shook his head as if *I* had the nerve to challenge *him*. Me. The new kid. A pipsqueak.

The chants grew louder.

"Nero!"

"Nero!"

"Nero!"

He smiled. He knew they all followed him out of fear. Most, if not all, of the kids had once felt the force of his fists and the power of his pure meanness.

I do not think any of the kids, except Sammy, knew my name. Nor did they care. I was simply some kid that was about to become one of them, one of Nero's victims.

I looked at Sammy. He shook and cried. He wiped tears off of his glasses. It struck me as odd that he cared so much, or maybe he did not care. Maybe he was scared, scared for himself or maybe for me or maybe for everyone. Sammy cried even though I stood there not yet harmed. I guess I could have backed out and run away. Perhaps this would have satisfied Nero without him needing to deliver a single blow. Perhaps not.

Nero circled me like a wildcat circling its prey. Then he stepped forward and drew a line in the dirt with his foot and spit on it. I had never seen someone do that before but I knew exactly what it meant.

The entire circle of kids became quiet.

I stepped across the line.

The roar was deafening. It shook the field and the trees and everyone on it.

Where were the teachers! Surely an adult somewhere could see and hear this horrible spectacle and intervene.

The roar and the mass of people did not bring help, but instead, they did the opposite—they isolated Nero and me from the rest of the world. To us, no other world mattered if it fell outside of that circle of children. No rules applied, except for the law of survival. No humans mattered, except for Nero and me.

There I stood, about to get my ass kicked by a man-child who feared nothing. On that playground, Nero ruled.

And he wasted no time in exercising his authority. He rushed at me and picked me up and threw me to the ground. I bounced back and rushed at him, only to be thrown on the ground again.

The crowd went wild. We might as well have been two wild animals in a death match—one was a battle-hardened lion and the other was me.

Later, much later, in high school, I joined the wrestling team. It was there I learned how to execute a lateral drop, which became my signature move. A lateral drop is perhaps the most exciting and game-changing move in wrestling. It happens when one wrestler in the standing position throws another wrestler, also in the standing position, to his back. It looks as if both wrestlers cut a synchronized flip in mid-air. Both completely leave their feet. But the wrestler performing the lateral drop ends up landing on top of the other wrestler who is being lateral dropped. It is beautiful. But it can only occur if all the right elements converge at the same time. One can only perform a lateral drop by using the momentum and force of the other wrestler. Imagine someone pushing against you and right as he pushes against you, you throw him behind you. If you miss the timing by a split-second, you lose. The other person falls on you and buries you in his weight, but if you time it just right, a small person can throw a huge person across a room. The more momentum, the harder the throw.

During the playground fight, I was holding my own with Nero in the sense that I was still alive and had not yet broken any bones. But he was hell-bent on changing that and the crowd loved it. After throwing me down one final time, he stood up and looked at me and smiled as if he had been toying with me all along. He looked at his crowd. They roared. He had done this before. They knew what this meant. He was going for the final kill and there would be no mercy. No one messed with Nero.

I stood up and brushed the dirt and blood and sweat out of my eyes. I saw him right before the final charge. He was a child but also a man—an evil, empty man. I saw the furious joy in his eyes. Then he charged. Right as he launched his body into mine, I turned, executing what was perhaps the finest lateral drop ever performed. We both flew to the edge of the crowd. And I landed on top. I felt his body go limp. Confused, I stood up and peered over him.

The crowd went silent.

Then one of the kids said, "Oh my God. He's dead! Nero's dead!"

The bell rang. Nero awoke. Everyone stood there stunned or scared or something. Nero looked around, also confused. Then a few people snickered and he realized what had happened. He looked at me and sneered, a mean, evil sneer. His eyes were empty. He shook his head, telling me that we would meet again.

We never fought again at school. He continued to bully other kids and I never challenged him again. A part of me knew that some things were better left alone.

Later, I discovered that Nero lived in a neighborhood near ours. Ours was a neighborhood of sorts—it was a dirt road with about five houses. A large wooded area separated my neighborhood from his. Enough woods that I did not see Nero in our neighborhood until the sixth grade.

By the sixth grade, I had built a magnificent tree house. It had taken more than three years to construct. But it was worth it. The tree house represented my entire life's work and I was proud of it. Not one adult had hammered a single nail. It was kid built. We loved it. We hunted in it. We slept in it. The tree house had two stories and a deck. It rested about twenty feet up above the ground, connected to five different trees. We had taken carpet out of an old van and laid it down on the first floor, the sleeping quarters. We had built a tent-like roof that could be rolled up and down so that we could stay dry during the rain. During deer season, I would dress up in warm camouflage, climb the tree house, and hunt deer with my BB gun. I never saw a deer and I really do not know what I would have done if I had seen a deer, but that did not matter. I was hunting out of my own tree house. No other achievement had given me more pride and sense of accomplishment than that tree house. To this day, it remains that way in my mind.

On one perfect, frosty morning, I walked through the woods to my tree house, only to find it completely destroyed and scattered about the ground.

It felt like someone had punched me in the stomach and then hit me with a car. I was distraught, in shock, and in pain. What happened? How could my tree house just fall apart in pieces? There had been no storm. Nothing that could have caused such damage. I looked about the debris and found ax marks. It was clear that someone had destroyed my tree house.

I cried as hard as a young boy could cry and I went home and told my parents what had happened. They were also confused.

"Son, I don't know what happened," Dad said. "Is there anyone you know that would do this?"

"No, Dad," I said. "No one."

Later that day, I learned that Nero lived nearby, not far away across the woods. I learned because I saw him in our woods, Nero and two other silhouettes. They were patrolling the area around my tree house, waiting for me.

When I saw them, I felt alone and scared. I was a child! But I decided to confront them anyway. When I got there, they all had guns—real guns, not the BB gun I had taken with me so many times.

"I heard somebody tore your tree house down," Nero said.

"That's right," I said.

"That's a shame," he said. "It takes a real mean person to do that to a kid."

I just looked at him. I felt so mad. I wanted to kill him. I might have killed him had it been in my power. But they had guns and I knew enough to know that he wanted me to confront him, to accuse him, to provoke him. He wanted me to rush him. That is why they were there and I am convinced, to this day, that he would have shot me dead had I charged.

"Let's go, guys," he said, realizing that I was not going to do anything.

Nero and the two silhouettes walked away. I stood there until they were almost out of sight. Then I followed, at a distance, right to the edge of the woods near Nero's house. That is when I saw it—another tree house. It was Nero's tree house. I had not even known he lived nearby, but there it was, what was left of it anyway. Most of it was scattered about the ground.

I know for a fact that Nero destroyed my tree house. I never saw him do it. No one ever told me he did it. Some things can be deduced with absolute certainty, without corroboration from eye-witness testimony or first-hand knowledge. To this day, I know who wrecked my tree house, but I have no idea who wrecked his. I am sure he thought it was me.

Nero and I always kept a safe distance away from each other and never met again until high school. He had failed a grade, so we were both seniors at rival schools.

Against all odds, Nero made it to his senior year. His dad was a drunk. His mom was a drunk. And they had always let him run wild, especially when Nero grew too big for his dad to hit and kick.

Outside of criminal activity, Nero did only one thing well—wrestling. He was an excellent wrestler. This was in no part due to his work ethic. Other than taking steroids on a regular basis, he never practiced or trained or did anything to better himself as a wrestler. But he was mean and strong and that was enough to be good.

The law eventually caught up with Nero. During wrestling season and much of his senior year, Nero faced charges of animal cruelty and vandalism. But because the judicial process was slow, Nero remained on the roster all season.

During one incident, Nero and another student, John Anderson, broke into a church playground after they had been smoking dope and drinking heavy amounts of alcohol. Nero and John systematically tore apart the playground. While vandalizing the church, they found a litter of puppies. This was too much of a temptation for Nero. He picked the puppies up, one by one, and punted them onto the roof of the church.

Nero would have burned the church down just for the hell of it had someone not seen him and run him off. The police were notified.

Before the police arrived, the pastor of the church came to Nero's house and knocked on his door. Nero's dad answered.

"Are you Judd Nero's father?" the pastor asked. "If so, then I need to speak with you for a few minutes."

"I don't want anything. Go away," Judd's dad said.

"It's not about you, it's about your son, Judd."

"What about him?"

Judd was in a room nearby and could hear every word.

"Well, sir, our playground was destroyed today," the pastor said.

"It wasn't him," Judd's dad said.

"Someone saw your son do it. They chased him away."

"It wasn't him. He didn't do it. You hear me, preacher? Now leave!"

"Mr. Nero, we also found newborn puppies on the roof."

"I said he didn't do it. Leave! Now!"

"I'm sorry you feel this way," the pastor said and left.

Judd's dad went over to Judd and said, "See what kind of trouble you cause me. You ain't worth a damn and never have been. Now I don't need any more damn preachers showing up at my door. You understand!"

"Yeah, Dad," Judd said.

"Don't call me Dad! Get out of my sight."

The pastor went to John's house.

"Mr. Anderson, I need to speak to you for a minute," the pastor said.

"What is it?" Mr. Anderson asked.

"Today our church playground was destroyed."

"Yes?"

"Your son was involved."

"You can stop right there."

"But Mr. Anderson . . ."

"Sir, I'll handle this. I'm sorry that this happened. Tomorrow morning, I will be at your church. And so will John. He is going to apologize to you in person. I'll give him the night to think about what he did, but tomorrow morning we are going to rebuild that playground. Every bit of it."

I do not recall John ever hanging out with Nero again and I never heard of John getting into trouble again.

Both my high school and Nero's high school had excellent wrestling teams. Both teams expected to wrestle against each other twice, once during the regular season and again during the state championship.

I had never wrestled until high school. The wrestling coach hounded me until I joined the team. He saw potential in my attitude, I think. The problem, however, was that I had no idea what I was doing and was a terrible wrestler. This meant that I spent the first two years getting beat up, every day at practice and during actual matches. Fortunately, the guys beating me up during practice were really good. Most of them had won a state championship. It was this experience, I think, that led to my success. By my senior year, South Carolina ranked me number one in the state in the 152-pound weight class.

Nero weighed about 250 pounds but wrestled in the 189-pound weight class. Wrestlers were known to cut weight, but not that much. He cheated and everyone knew it.

Nero was nothing but pure muscle. He had used steroids since the seventh grade. Everyone knew he used steroids but did nothing about it.

Our schools met once during the regular season. It was unusual for any small town to have two top teams. So the meeting between the two rivals became the main event of the year, no less important, in that town anyway, than a world-championship fight in Las Vegas.

The gym was packed. There were no empty spaces in the bleachers. Elderly men and women brought their own chairs and placed them around the mat. Others simply stood the entire time.

As expected, I weighed in at just over 152 pounds.

"I need you to wrestle up tonight," my coach said.

"No problem," I said.

"Be ready to wrestle anywhere from 152 to 189."

"Got it."

I felt confident. I had developed into a good wrestler. I had trained hard and was ready for the match.

When the referee called for the 152-pound match, I remained seated. He called for the 160-pound match and I remained seated. The team score was almost tied.

Right before the 171-pound match, my coach came over to me.

"Mel, you're wrestling 189," he said.

"Got it," I said.

The fact that Nero wrestled 189 made it even sweeter. He was strong, but I was faster and I was ready for this.

Right before the 189-pound match, the score remained close. They led by one point.

My coach looked at me and said, "Just don't get pinned. You should win this, but the team can still win if you lose, as long as you don't get pinned."

The referee announced our match, "And at 189 pounds—Judd Nero and Melvin Scott!"

The gymnasium roared. This was Nero's moment. Judd was their best wrestler, but I was better.

I stood on the mat across from Nero. It did not get any better than this, I thought. From the beginning, I attacked and he proved to be no match. I moved too fast for him, especially when on my feet. Soon the score looked lopsided and I began taking him down to the mat at will. I would take him down and let him up and take him down and let him up. He was a big huge beast and it seemed as if I were toying with him.

The score remained lopsided into the third and final period. With thirty seconds left on the clock, I took him down one last time. But before I let him up he grabbed my leg and I fell to the mat. He fell on top of me. I was on my back! I panicked. What happened! It had been years since I had been on my back. Then I felt him clamp down with every bit of strength he possessed. In seconds, it was over.

The referee slapped his hand on the mat. The crowd roared. I had been pinned.

Driving home alone, I yelled and cursed and yelled and cursed until I pulled into my driveway. How did I let this happen! How did I lose! To Judd Nero of all people! I was so mad, so mad at myself, and I never forgot it.

The loss stood as my only loss during the regular season, but I would have traded ten losses to have that match back. Then playoffs began.

I still find it amazing that I have forgotten so much about high school, but I remember every single detail of the state championship match, our final match. I remember the warm yellow color of the lights in the gymnasium. I remember the smell of fresh rubber on the mat. I remember the faces of thousands of people that had piled in that gym to watch our schools square off.

An unusual number of people attended that night, more so than any prior state championship. It was a rivalry. It was a state championship. But more so than anything, there had been a fight during the semi-finals match between Nero's school and another school. Everyone expected a fight to break out between our schools.

The fight during the semi-finals match happened during the 189-pound match, but it was not a fight among the wrestlers. The crowd had turned on each other.

It all started after Nero's mom slapped the scorekeeper, a middle-school child no older than twelve. During Nero's match, the kid got the score wrong, giving the other wrestler an extra point. It was not on purpose and could have been corrected easily.

Nero's mom saw it. She had never been to a wrestling match, but she knew enough to know that the boy got the score wrong. So she went down to the scorekeeper's table and slapped the boy in his face. Then the stands collapsed and the crowd fought each other almost at random.

During the week leading up to the state championship, word spread quickly in the halls. Students who cared nothing about wrestling or about winning a state championship in anything planned to watch the match. Everyone would be there. There is something about a fight—a real fight—that draws humans to it.

"There will be no fighting at the match!" our coach told us. "Absolutely none!"

We got it. None of us wanted a dumb fight anyway. We were wrestlers, not street fighters. We had worked hard for this and wanted to win the right way and cared nothing for a gym brawl.

Both towns showed up to the match. It began with the gym bursting at its seams.

I weighed in at 152 pounds.

"Mel, I need you to wrestle up tonight," my coach said.

"No problem," I said.

I understood, but this time there was a problem. For two days, I had not held any food down, not because I was cutting weight but because I was sick. Bad sick. I should have told my coach, but this was the state championship and my last match ever.

Only my dad knew how sick I was.

"Dad, I don't know what I'm going to do," I said.

"Well, maybe you should sit this one out," Dad said.

"I can't do that. You know that."

"I know."

"I'm sick. Real sick. I can't last for three periods, with anyone."

"Son," he said. "This is your decision. Only you can make it. No matter what you decide, I understand."

Dad could not find room to sit on our side of the gym so he found a seat on the other side. At some point in time, right before the 189-pound match, Nero's mom came down and sat beside my dad.

It turned out that the 189-pound match would be the last match. That was how the order played out. It started with heavy weights and then moved to the 103-pound class and then up from there, ending with the 189-pound match.

I felt the inevitable. I knew which match I would wrestle. Like two asteroids heading toward one another, there are some things in this world that are in motion on a collision course and there is nothing anyone can do to stop those things from colliding. Their course cannot be altered. This proved true that night.

When the 189-pound match began, the team score was tied. I had suspected it would be this way. I feared it. I felt so sick. I sat still in my chair as Nero paced back and forth on the other side, staring at me.

I felt almost too sick to care, but there was so much at stake.

No fight had broken out even though Nero's entire clan sat in the stands. Even his dad showed up. I do not think any of them cared about Nero. Almost all of them, including his dad, had never attended a match. But Nero's mom had kicked some boy's ass last week and they were not going to miss this one.

"Your son is going to get it now!" Nero's mom yelled in my dad's ear.

Dad just sat there.

"Mr. I'm-ranked-number-one-in-the-state is going to get his ass kicked! Just like last time!"

Dad just sat there.

The referee announced the final match, "And at 189 pounds—Judd Nero and Melvin Scott!"

We met in the middle of the mat in the middle of the roaring crowd in what seemed like a very bad dream. We shook hands, but only because the rules required it. Everyone stood on their feet. This was it. The final match. Everything was tied.

My teammates stood on their feet. They knew I could and should beat Nero. They all knew that my last loss was a fluke.

I shot at Nero in a half attempt to take him down. He dodged me. I did not actually want to grab his massive legs or waist. I knew I could not take him down in my condition. But I did not want to get penalized for stalling and I did not want him to know that I felt sick and faint. I had just enough energy to dodge his lumbering shots but each effort sucked gas out of my already empty tank.

The first period ended with no score. My side hurt. My stomach hurt. I felt cottonmouth in my throat. The crowd's roar grew louder and louder, reverberating about the gym walls. My teammates, however, stayed silent. They had sat back down. They sat confused. They knew something was terribly wrong. I normally wrestled best on my feet.

I had failed to score a single point.

I felt sick. I felt like vomiting, but I had nothing to vomit. I had no plan, not even one of desperation. I just knew that I had to stay on my feet and away from Nero's grip.

The second period began with no score.

At the beginning of the second and third period, a wrestler gets to choose top, bottom, or neutral. One always chooses bottom, because the wrestler gets one point for escaping from the bottom. We were tied. One point would likely win this match. It was the second period and it was my choice.

"Neutral," I said, baffling the referee, my team, and everyone else in the gymnasium. Neutral meant we both started on our feet. I knew Nero was too strong and I too weak for me to choose bottom. Nero would have squeezed the life out of me.

The crowd roared. The whole gym began to shake, especially Nero's side. My teammates put their faces in their hands. My coach stood there in disbelief. Nero's mom rattled off obscenities at my dad.

Dad just sat there.

Nero became more and more confident. We circled and made half-attempts at taking each other down. He knew I was fast and I knew I was sick.

The second period ended with no score.

The crowd was now jumping up and down, adding to the already deafening roar and vibration. The entire building threatened to collapse. No one cared. This was the third and final period of the final match between the last two remaining teams in the state tournament.

It was the third period and Nero's choice. As expected, he chose bottom.

As a spectator at other events, I have never heard or felt or experienced energy like the energy I felt in that gym. I have been at football stadiums where over ninety thousand people roared and jumped and shouted and screamed in wild rhythm before the last play of a final game in overtime. No such experience ever produced more energy than that high school gymnasium during those final seconds.

The referee blew his whistle. I started on top. I knew I could not hold Nero, so I let him up, pushing him to the edge of the ring. 1 to 0. Nero's first point. The crowd went wild.

I did not mean to push Nero so hard, but it looked like I had pushed him out of disgust or disrespect. I think it looked this way because he exploded off the bottom and I did nothing to prevent it.

Nero's kin went nuts. Nero's crowd went nuts. Everyone in the gym seemed to lose their sanity all at the same time. My teammates sat silent, beside themselves with confusion and despair. I felt sick. All he had to do now was stand there and let time expire. All hope faded. I stood alone in the middle of the mat, knowing it would all be over soon.

Sweat stung my eyes and I felt the room closing in, getting dimmer and dimmer. I had passed out many times before when exhaustion took over. I felt it taking over my body then. The end neared. I could no longer hear the crowd but I knew it roared on. Wiping the sweat from my eyes, I saw Nero glaring at me. He shook his head. I saw the furious joy in his eyes. The crowd erupted. Then he charged. Right as he launched his body into mine, I executed what was perhaps the second-finest lateral drop ever performed. We both flew to the edge of the mat. I landed on top and felt his body go limp.

"One, two, three!" the referee slapped his hand on the mat. Pinned.

My dad turned to Nero's mom.

"Yep, that's what he said he was going to do."

Then Dad got up and left.

The crowd on both sides collapsed in hysteria. In the chaos, one of my teammates took me off the mat and we escaped with the rest of our team through back doors in the gym. The crowd got their fight while we privately celebrated away from it all. I lay next to a toilet and dry-heaved until I passed out.

While standing on the bluff at the marina, I stared at Charcoal's yacht and across the marsh. How could that monster have returned to my life? It was too much. The sight of him brought back the pain and disgust I had felt as a child. I could not believe he was here, near my family's new home. Let them find a billion dollars in gold. It was not worth it. I turned around and went back to The Wreck.

CHAPTER 19

## *Danny's Reveal Party*

D anny and Wendy Ann were visiting with us for the weekend. Lynn had told Wendy Ann that she was pregnant, so they went off to discuss their plans for the next eighteen years of our unborn child's life, which began with decorating the nursery.

Danny and I went to see if there were any good games on television.

"Hey, man. I got a surprise for you," Danny said.

"Should I be worried right now? Is it inside the house?"

"Naw, man. See, I had an idea the other day."

"Well, that is a surprise."

"What we should do is have a reveal."

"A reveal? What is that?"

"A reveal. You know. A reveal party. Someone makes a cake and the inside is either blue or pink. We all get together and you cut the cake. You find out whether you're getting a little baby girl or little baby boy. Then we party."

"Interesting. I'll talk to Lynn. She might actually like your idea."

"Well, dang, that idea ain't mine. People do it all the time. My idea is in the cake."

The doorbell rang. It was Ms. Mable, one of my neighbors. She was holding a large bag.

"Hi, Ms. Mable," I said.

"Hello," she said.

Ms. Mable's age fell somewhere between seventy-five and eighty. I knew little about her except that she had lived alone for the past twenty years.

"Have you seen Otis's cat lately?" she asked.

"As a matter of fact, I have not. He has been looking for it."

"That is because it was at my house."

"That's great. I'll tell Otis. He'll be glad to know."

"Yes, please do. And take this bag with you."

I looked in the bag and Otis's cat jumped out and onto my shoulder.

"Thank you, Ms. Mable," I said. "Danny, I'll be right back and you can tell me more about this reveal party."

I left Danny with Ms. Mable and walked next door to Otis's. We had not told our neighbors that Lynn was pregnant. We had only told close family members, which unfortunately included Danny.

"A reveal party. What is that?" Ms. Mable asked Danny.

"Hi, ma'am. I'm Danny. Mel's brother-in-law. I married his sister."

"Nice to meet you, Danny. Do you live nearby?" she asked.

"Sort of. There is nothing nearby here. We're in Savannah. Just visiting today. Trying to convince Mel to throw a reveal party."

"Oh my, I love parties. What is a reveal party?"

"What is a reveal party! Why it just happens to be the best party ever! No kids, just adults. The little ones would not understand anyway."

"Sounds intriguing."

"Oh, there's lots of intrigue. That's the whole point of the party."

"Oh, please tell me more."

"Well, what we do is get all the men and women together. Just close friends and family, you know. People who can keep a secret."

"Very interesting."

"See here, nobody but me and a few others know exactly what the sex is going to be."

"Oh my!"

"That's right. But see, at least one person, maybe two or three are in on it."

"Oh, that is interesting. Did you say three?"

"Well, just in the beginning. Then we get everyone involved, except Lynn and Mel of course."

"Oh, yes, of course. I would not expect them to be involved."

"We have some drinks and fool around for a while and act like it ain't no big deal."

"Oh, this is so scandalous."

"Yeah, it really builds up the anticipation if you do it just right."

"Oh, Danny, you're making me dizzy!"

"When everyone is in just the right state of intoxication, which means I'm drunk, the show begins."

"Oh my! Danny boy! Please stop!"

"Here's the best part. They think it is going to be some long, drawn-out ordeal. Not this year. Not with Danny boy."

"Danny, this is too much."

"This year it's going to be like, BAAM! I surprise them all of a sudden with a great big climax. Then we party."

"Oh dear! Jesse was that way too!"

"Jesse. Who's Jesse?"

"Oh, nobody. Was a friend until he ran off with that devil woman."

"Anyway, you should come. Shoot, I could use some help. My wife doesn't exactly approve of my plans. It will be more fun to do it with other people anyway."

"Really, Danny. Me? I don't know."

"Sure, it's no work for you. I'll take care of all the hard stuff. Just maybe bring some toys. Not many clothes though. And please, don't bring any diapers."

"Why, of course, I will leave mine at home."

After I returned from Otis's, I did not have time to get all the details from Danny about his reveal party but agreed to host it anyway. I was somewhat concerned about Danny's idea. In part because he did not have many ideas and in part because the few he had usually resulted in damage to something or someone, often me.

We agreed to let him throw a reveal party at our house. He showed up to the reveal party with a large, odd-shaped cake.

"Danny, is that the cake?" I asked.

"Better not touch it," Danny said. "Of course it's the cake. But I'm not sure how stable the explosives are."

"Explosives!"

"Yeah, man, this here is a bomb. Made it myself."

"What!"

"Idea was all mine too. Got it from right here," he said, pointing at his head. "And a little bit from the internet."

"Lord help us."

"Now see. What you're looking at is about fifty pounds of nitrate reloading powder. Hit it with a shotgun blast and BOOM! You know if you're having a little baby girl or a little baby boy. Filled it with colored flour. That part was all my idea."

"Ok. Uh, thanks."

"You're welcome, brother. Where's the booze?"

Many of our family members arrived. Ms. Mable showed up early. She followed Danny around the room like a little puppy dog. There was something about her that seemed out of place, besides her unusual attraction to Danny.

"Nice party, Son," Dad said.

"Thanks," I said.

"Who is that older lady?" Dad asked.

"Ms. Mable, she's a little off."

"I would say so. Does she always wear lingerie around the neighbors?"

"I hope not."

"Attention everyone!" Danny shouted. "Attention everyone!"

"He has a gun!" someone screamed.

"I don't know what my daughter ever saw in him," Dad said.

"Attention everyone! I would like to raise a toast," Danny said.

Danny raised his shotgun.

"Danny!" Dad said. "Can we do this outside?"

"Sure, Dad," Danny said. "Good idea."

We all went outside and Danny rambled on about the process of making a homemade bomb and how he was not sure if he got the mixture just right but doubled the amount of gunpowder just to be safe.

Then he turned to me and said, "And here, brother, all you have to do is fire this here shotgun into the cake."

I looked at Lynn.

"Honey, maybe you should go around the house," I said.

Lynn and a few of the more responsible family members went around the house. Lynn peeked around the corner as I raised the gun.

"How far back should I stand?" I asked Danny.

"I don't know. A few feet I guess."

"Maybe we should use a rifle instead. I could get a little farther back and . . ."

"Just fire the damn gun!" Danny said.

The mushroom cloud was visible thirty miles away. Most of the windows in my house shattered. A huge crater appeared where my new sod once lay. We lost several large trees. The tires on my van went flat. When my hearing returned, I could hear the sirens on their way.

The cleanup was going to be expensive. I did not have time to deal with it myself. Nor did I have the money to hire someone else. I lay against the side of my house in silence, unable to even think about the extent of the damage. I was too busy smiling at the beautiful pink mess.

CHAPTER 20

# *Fireball*

There is something sacred about Saturdays for the working parent. There is no need to fight traffic on the way to work. No need to cart kids to school. No need to do anything in particular.

"Let's take the boat out today," Dad said early one Saturday morning.

"Ok. To where?" I asked.

"I don't know, maybe head toward Blackbeard Island. There are some places I have not seen in forty years. I wonder if they are still there."

"I'll see if Lynn can watch the kids."

My mom and dad had come down for Danny's reveal party and decided to stay the weekend with us. Mom and Lynn sat at the dining room table flipping through a magazine and looking at what appeared to be children's clothes on the computer.

"What is this?" I asked.

"A magazine," Lynn said. "We're shopping for baby girl clothes."

"Don't we have a lot of baby girl clothes already?" I asked.

"Yes, but those are Sophia's. We need some for her sister."

"Oh."

"And we need to decorate her sister's room."

"Oh."

"And we will need to get matching clothes for both of them."

"Oh."

"Do you need something from us?" Lynn asked.

"Dad wants to take the boat out," I said.

"Oh," Lynn said.

"He needs me to go with him."

"Oh."

"We might be gone all day."

"Oh."

"You and your father go and enjoy the day," Mom said. "I'll help watch the kids."

"Thank you," I said.

"We will just stay here and shop until you get back," Mom said.

"Ok," I said. "Well, the weather might turn bad, so it is possible we are only gone for a few hours."

"No need to rush," Lynn said.

"I think there is a tornado warning," I said.

"Try not to get too close," she said.

"Now that I think about it, it might be better if Dad and I just fish off the bank for a few minutes," I said.

"You'll be fine," Lynn said.

"Ok," I said. "Just please remember to be very careful while I'm gone."

"Stop worrying so much. Go," she said.

I went outside and got in Dad's truck.

"Let's go for a long ride on the water," Dad said. "I packed everything yesterday."

An old boatlift at the marina hoisted Dad's boat off the trailer and eased it into the river. The orange and golden sun slowly rose in the distance, reflecting across the calm waters. We rode away with a steady current, heading south through winding water on our way to Blackbeard Island.

"This marsh raised me, Son," Dad said. "Growing up, I spent more days on this marsh than at home. I used to know every square inch of it. Over forty years have passed and I still remember every fishing hole and every oyster bed. I know where I could find clams and shrimp and anything else a person could want from the marsh. Over forty years have passed and this marsh is still more of a home than anywhere else."

"I guess it's a good thing I moved down here," I said.

"No. It's not."

"What do you mean? I thought you loved this place."

"I do, more than anywhere else, but I left for a reason. I raised you somewhere else for a reason."

"I don't understand."

"Son, this place ain't normal. There is something about this place that I just can't explain because I don't know how. It is wild and strange and might as well be another planet. There is a force about it that sucks you in like gravity. Don't think for one minute that you are here by accident."

"Well, I'm stuck here now."

"I know. That is why I'm showing you the marsh. There are things you need to know, for your sake and your children's sake."

"Like what?"

"My grandfather is buried somewhere out in that mud. Do you know how he died?"

"It was a hunting accident, right?"

"That was what everyone said happened, that he was shot in the stomach with a shotgun by accident. That was what his friends said and it might be true. Either way, he sank to the bottom like a rock and we have never seen him since. I was eight when that happened. Do you want to know why he died?"

I nodded.

"He was reckless, that was why he died. This place makes you reckless to the point where you think reckless is normal. It is just the way it is. My dad is buried in this marsh too. Do you know how he died?"

"I think he died from a heart attack or a stroke or both."

"No. He died from recklessness. He lived a reckless life. He drank hard and he smoked hard and he lived hard without any regard to his own health. He loved this marsh too and we spread his ashes across it, just like he asked us to do. This place is like some damned beautiful curse."

"I see."

"And someday you are going to do the same for me, but not anytime soon, you hear. I am the oldest Scott man in the family and I don't plan on going away anytime soon."

"That's good to hear."

"Do you understand what I'm telling you?"

"I think so."

"I don't think you do, but you will learn. You have to learn because you live in it now!"

I nodded. I could tell he was getting upset.

"You are up to your neck in debt on a house and a van and you have two children and another on the way and there's little hope for good employment," he said, still upset but trying to calm down. "Look, I'm sorry, just try to see it from where I am. I left this place for a reason and never intended on coming back. Then out of the blue, you moved down here. Less than twenty-four hours after you arrived here, you nearly died. We almost lost you! Do you understand! I did not rush down here to bury my son, you understand?"

"I'm sorry."

"There is no reason to be sorry. It's not your fault. I thought it was at first, or that maybe it was mine, but it's not your fault. It is this damned marsh, this beautiful, cursed marsh. It sucks you in and makes you forget about the rest of the world, the real world. I want you to understand it, even if I can't explain it. That is one reason why we are out here now."

We had traveled many miles away from the marina. Marsh and water and islands surrounded us in every direction as far as one could see. There were no boats, no houses, no signs of human activity, except for the small wake behind our boat.

"Where are we going?" I asked.

"It's a special place. We called it the Mullet Hole. That was our code name for it."

"Are we going fishing there?"

"Fishing! No, Son. You don't go fishing in the Mullet Hole. You go harvesting."

"Yeah?"

"After you experience it, you'll understand and you'll know why you must keep it secret forever. This place is like no other and no one else knows about it."

"I thought you said, we used to call it the Mullet Hole."

"There was one other who knew about it, but he must be dead by now. I have not seen or heard from him in over forty years and I know he would have kept it a secret."

"So, what is so special about the Mullet Hole?" I asked.

"It is full of fish and shrimp and crab and anything else you could want from the sea. It is full of food, every single day, at low tide. It makes fishing seem like a silly game. I'm telling you, Son, this place is an underwater Garden of Eden. You can pluck fish out of it like picking apples and there's no work involved. One can throw his net once and have food for the week. It's an underwater miracle. It's a deep hole at the intersection of five large tidal creeks. At low tide, the water dumps thousands of fish and shrimp and crabs in it and they stay trapped until the incoming tide takes them back into the grass. A man could live off the Mullet Hole for life and feed his family too. That's one reason why I'm showing you the place. It is my backup plan and it will be yours too. When this economy crumbles, and it will, you will have the Mullet Hole and it will provide for you for as long as you need it, but only if it is kept a secret. Humans will ruin it just like they ruin everything. If the wrong person—which is almost everyone—finds out about it, then the underwater Garden of Eden will disappear and be gone forever. That cuts both ways. Like the marsh, the Mullet Hole can ruin you. It can suck you in. I used to dream about living on a boat and never having to work. I dreamed of living off the Mullet Hole because I knew it was possible. But a man should work and there is more to life than food, but if all you needed was food, the Mullet Hole would provide. We're almost there. See that island up ahead? It is behind that island, tucked away in a cove."

We eased behind the island and saw a sailboat anchored in the cove. It was a small sailboat with tiny glass portholes on the side.

"I thought you said no one knew about it."

"I guess I was wrong. Maybe this person is lost. They are either lost or know exactly what they are doing here. Only a fool or an expert would sail a boat against these tides in this creek. We'll ease up to them and see if they need any help."

"Hello!" Dad yelled. "Do you need any help?"

A man opened the small cabin door and stood up in the cockpit.

"No," said the man. "I'm, uh, lost, but doing fine. I'm just waiting for the tide to rise so I can get out of here."

"I know that voice," Dad said. "But it can't be him."

"Who?" I asked.

We eased closer, now just a few feet away.

"I'll be damned. Jesse Turner!"

"Is that you Junior? Sure as hell is."

The two men almost fell into the water as they scrambled to hug each other.

"Damned if it ain't you, Jesse. I took you for dead years ago."

"I haven't given up yet. How long has it been? Forty years?"

"At least."

"Is this your son?"

"Yes," Dad said. "Mel, come meet Jesse."

"He is a spitting image, Junior, a spitting image."

"How's the Mullet Hole?" Dad asked.

"It hasn't changed. Not one bit. I have been living off of it for forty years and you're the first person I have seen here. Mel, can you believe your dad showed this place to me when we were boys. He showed me everything because he knew everything about this marsh. So did his daddy, Senior. When we were young boys, Hugh Sr. would put us in his truck and drag us down here while he went off fishing, but we knew he just went off in the boat drinking, him and all the other men down here. That was fine because it gave us complete freedom to do whatever we wanted. What was that fish camp we stayed at called?"

"Hoffman's," Dad said.

"That's it, Hoffman's. A German couple ran it. Mrs. Hoffman was the only human being who cared about what we did. She was always looking after us and always yelling at Senior."

"Yeah, it was a different time," Dad said.

"Different is not the word. Mel, did your dad ever tell you about the time he fell off the dock from that high bluff?" Jesse asked.

"No," I said.

"Jesse, he doesn't need to know about all this," Dad said.

"There was a dock on the edge of the bluff. I think the bluff was thirty or forty feet high with two big floating docks on the water. It didn't matter. Junior rolled right off of the high dock and right into the black water. How old were you?"

"Five years old," Dad said.

"That sounds right. Junior was always getting into trouble, nothing mean, just reckless. He was reckless as the day is old."

"Jesse, that's enough," Dad said.

"No," I said. "Please continue."

"Old Man Hoffman and his wife were good people. The best. I don't think they make them like that anymore. Mr. Hoffman was as stout and sturdy as they come. He had the broadest shoulders and burliest arms I had ever seen. The only person stronger than Mr. Hoffman was Mrs. Hoffman. They owned the fish camp and she ran it. Nobody crossed Mrs. Hoffman, nobody but Senior, and he only did so when he was drunk, which was most of the time. Every day she threatened to kick him out of the fish camp, but Senior had an ace and he knew it. That woman had a heart that was soft as mud for Junior. She loved us, but I think she loved Junior more than anything else in the world. What was that she called you? Some German name."

"Dummkoph," Dad said.

"That's right, Dummkoph. You were her little Dummkoph. Man, the memories are racing back now. I remember that night Junior almost died as if it were last night. It was dusk and there was a full moon. The sun was setting and the moon was rising at the same time. It was orange and gold and yellow in every direction, right before it turned dark. We were standing on the high bluff, looking for Senior, waiting to see all those big trout Senior was known to catch. Junior saw him coming toward us and ran down the dock. He tripped and fell headfirst down into that black, glittering water. It sucked him down like a black hole. There was an ebb tide and the current was fast. None of us knew what to do. We looked for him, hoping he would pop up somewhere, but he never did."

Jesse looked at me and then continued, "Your dad and I were supposed to be fishing with Senior all week. But we were down to one boat on account of the storm. The day before, we had been on the marsh in one of Hoffman's wooden boats. Hoffman had made those boats himself and was proud of them too. I think the only reason he let us take one of his boats was because Dummkoph was with us. It was me, Junior, Senior, and Senior's brother. And man did we ever get into the trout that day! They were thick and biting like there was no tomorrow, probably because they knew a big storm was rolling in and thought there was no tomorrow. When the storm hit us, the tide dropped and we got stuck on a mud bar. We were miles away from camp and I was certain it was the end for all of us. I think everyone felt that way but the Hoffman's. They were not just tough and kind, they were smart. Mrs. Hoffman saw the storm long before we did. She knew that the storm would hit when the tide was dropping and that it would turn dark soon and that we were a boat full of idiots, so she immediately told Mr. Hoffman to get in his other boat and bring us back. And, of course, he did. Meanwhile, all of us had given up hope, except for Senior. He was too drunk to know it was the end. Senior ordered us all out of the boat and onto the mud bar. We stood there wet and scared, knee deep in the marsh while Senior dumped his bottle of moonshine all over the wooden boat. I turned around and saw Mr. Hoffman in his boat coming to save us. He waved. I waved back. Senior yelled at all of us to stand back and then Senior waved his arms up and down to shake every ounce of alcohol onto Hoffman's wooden boat. Right as Mr. Hoffman pulled up, Senior lit a match and threw it on the boat. It burst into flames, knocking all of us back and burning Senior's eyebrows. He turned around grinning like an idiot, putting his hands on his hips as if he were going to save us all. Old Man Hoffman put us boys in his boat. He was shaking he was so mad, but he had not been able to say a word. Senior and his brother got in and thanked him and offered Old Man Hoffman a swig on a bottle of whiskey that Senior had kept in his back pocket. Old Man Hoffman took that bottle and threw it in the marsh. Still shaking, he looked at Senior and said, 'Ah, ah, I don't know why in the hell you had to, had to burn my Gahldamned boat!' Nobody said anything after that, even Senior and his brother stayed quiet. After we got back to the camp, Mrs. Hoffman threatened to kick Senior out of the camp for good and told him to leave the next morning. Well, the next day, Senior did leave. He packed up everything in his old truck and made sure we were dressed in our good pants as if we were going back to town. He told us to go tell Mr. and Mrs. Hoffman goodbye and thank you. Senior might have been reckless, but he was clever too. He sent us all dressed up just for show. While we were saying our goodbyes, Senior and his brother snuck off in Hoffman's one remaining wooden boat and went fishing. They both knew the trout were biting and just could not let it go. They left us boys at the camp. Senior and his brother stayed out all day. We figured they must have really been into the trout to wait until dusk to return. We didn't mind because that just gave us another day of freedom on the marsh. Mrs. Hoffman treated us well and even gave us candy. What was that piece of candy she gave you, Junior?"

"A fireball," Dad said.

"That's right, a fireball. It was a round, hard piece of candy that seemed to last forever. Well, right about dark, Senior and his brother tried to sneak up the creek, but they were too drunk and clumsy, making a foolish racket in Hoffman's boat. That's when Junior saw them. Everyone saw them. They kept running into the bank, nearly beating that old boat to pieces. Then it started to sink, so they jumped overboard and swam to the bank. That was right about the time Junior fell in. Mrs. Hoffman would have skinned Senior on the spot except she was too worried and sick about Junior. Everyone was sick. All hands stood on that dock, looking for Junior, but he never came up. With the full moon and a strong tide, that current was racing. Some of the fishermen scrambled to their boats to see if Junior had floated down the creek but there were no signs of him. There was a tall college boy at the camp that night. We found out later he was a big-time high diver. Man, if he didn't dive right off of that bluff and in between two of those big floating docks. I remember seeing him swimming back and forth under those long docks, popping up like a sea otter. I don't think another human being on the planet could have done it with the current the way it was. After about thirty minutes with no sign of Junior, that whole place was a nervous wreck. We all knew that Junior was dead and gone and Mrs. Hoffman was crying so, which caused all the men in the camp to cry and Senior was as white as a ghost and distraught. We all were, until that college boy popped up with Junior's body all wet and limp and blue and dangling from that college boy's arms. No one had ever seen that big strong woman cry before, but she was crying and praying as if a mother had just lost her only child. I think that is what Junior was to her. He was her little Dummkoph. That college boy did not waste a second. He laid Junior down and started pumping on his chest. It weren't less than thirty seconds and out pops a fireball. Junior wakes up and looks right at me. I remember exactly what he said. He said, 'Daddy is going to kill me.'"

"I was wearing my good pants," Dad said.

"Senior didn't waste any time. He threw Junior into the truck as quick as lightning and drove down that road with that big woman just a running after them. That's the way it happened."

"That sounds about right. I was knocked out for most of it," Dad said. "The doctor said the fireball saved my life. It got stuck in the back of my mouth when I was pinned under the floating dock. I must have been near an air pocket and the fireball acted like some kind of valve or something. But for that piece of candy, my lungs would have filled up with water."

"So, I guess that fireball saved you," Jesse said.

"No doubt about it. And I am thankful for it."

"That should make at least three of us," Jesse said. "None of us would be here right now, but for that piece of candy. I owe my way of life to that piece of candy and to you, Junior."

"How so?" Dad asked.

"You showed me this marsh. You showed me everything about this marsh and I've never left. I never had to work a regular job. I've lived about the best life a man can ask for."

"Well, you're welcome, I guess," Dad said.

We spent the rest of the day at the Mullet Hole. Dad and Jesse talked about the past sixty years while I listened. It was the most relaxed I had ever seen my father. He was at peace with Jesse and me that day on the marsh. When the sun began to set, we pulled anchor.

"It was good to see you, Jesse," Dad said.

"You too, Junior," Jesse said.

"I guess we'll see you around now that Mel lives here," Dad said.

"For sure," Jesse said, turning to me. "Mel, your dad is like a brother to me and I owe everything to him. You remember that. If you ever need anything around here, don't hesitate to ask."

"Thank you," I said, and we went back home.

CHAPTER 21

## *Lunch with Danny*

We needed a break. The house and kids were driving us crazy, so we decided to get away for the weekend and stay with Danny and Wendy Ann. Lynn took Tyler and Sophia to their house early on Friday while I went to work. Danny and I met up for lunch in downtown Savannah.

"Man, we're going to have a great weekend," Danny said.

"Thank you for letting us stay," I said.

"No problem. We just had a ton of work done and Wendy Ann wants to show the place to Lynn. Wendy Ann bought a bunch of new furniture and had all the interior walls painted."

"I don't even want to talk about home-improvement projects. My house will not leave me alone. Neither will my kids. It's like they have teamed up against me in some giant effort to drive me nuts. I don't know how working parents do it."

"Me neither," Danny said.

"That's because you don't work and you're not a parent!"

"That does make it easier," he said. "I hope you don't mind, but I invited someone to join us for lunch. There she is now."

"It is the lady from our last lunch," I said as she walked over to our table. "I think she lived on a rambling ranch or something."

"That's right. You met her already. Anyway, just don't ask about her husband. They are on rocky terms right now. I don't know what is going on and I don't want to."

"Got it."

"Hello, gentlemen," she said. "Thank you for inviting me to lunch."

"No problem," Danny said. "You remember Mel?"

"Yes," she said.

"Hello," I said. "It is good to see you again."

"And you," she said. "I apologize if I am not good company today. I am exhausted and a little out of sorts."

"It happens," I said. "I was just telling Danny how my kids are driving me crazy."

She nodded and continued to look at the menu. "If you'll excuse me for a second, I'll be right back."

She stood up and went to the ladies' room.

"So, what is going on with your house these days?" Danny asked.

"It is still trying to kill me."

"You have to take control of that situation, man," Danny said. "You can't spend the rest of your life fighting it."

The ranch house lady returned to her seat and picked up her menu.

"I know," I said. "We have not been together that long, but it feels like I have owned her for years."

"I know what you mean," Danny said.

"The honeymoon phase was short—too short—only a few hours it seemed. I mean, when I first saw her, I thought she was beautiful. Sure, she wasn't perfect and needed some work, but there was nothing a little tender loving care couldn't fix."

"That's what you thought anyway," Danny said.

The ranch lady looked up from her menu, but remained quiet, pretending not to listen.

"Yeah, she turned on me, real quick," I said.

"I remember that," Danny said.

"I wanted to talk to my wife about it."

"You were married?" she asked.

"Yes, still am," I said, turning back to Danny, "but I did not think my wife would understand. Men and women are just different. They have different priorities."

"You got that right," Danny said.

"I thought she would be easy and I could take care of her and my wife and my kids at the same time, but it is not working out that way."

"Why don't you just get rid of her? She's just a piece of property."

"I beg your pardon!" the ranch lady said.

"I know. I know," I said, "but I feel like there's more to it, that she's more than just a piece of real estate. I feel like she is worth hanging on to for now."

"I guess. That's your decision, man."

"It is different with kids."

"You have children too!" she said.

"Yes," I said, turning back to Danny, "kids make the situation much more complicated. If I'm honest with myself, my wife and my kids are not the main problem."

"Then what's the problem?" Danny asked.

"I don't know how to say this any other way, but I am afraid that if I get rid of her and move on, then the next one I get will be even more of a bitch than the one I own now." That did it. Something set her off. The ranch lady jumped out of her chair, glared at me and Danny and screamed at us both, "So you are just going to move on to the next one! To some other bitch, you call her! Some other bitch for you to own! You are terrible, horrible, no-good, filthy pigs! Both of you and all of your kind should be ashamed, but that is not possible because you are incapable of feeling shame! I never, ever want to see or hear from either one of you again!"

She stormed off, leaving Danny and me speechless.

"Strange," Danny said. "I guess she really loves houses."

"Might be hormones," I said. "I've seen this sort of thing before. She will realize how out-of-line she was and want to apologize for making a scene and probably feel very embarrassed. Next time you see her, please let her know I understand and that I did not take any offense."

"Will do. You're probably right. But I am not going to bring it up unless she does, just in case she is too embarrassed. Anyway, I think I can help you solve this house problem. Tell me about the last time you had a problem with the house."

"Do you want to hear about the dried boogers or the dead squirrels?"

"Hmm. Let's go with dried boogers first."

"Sure. I was coming home from work the other day when I saw dried boogers on the front door. I was exhausted and you know how I hate my job. I had spent the whole day filling out reports for my boss. He wanted to know why my team was always complaining. So I had everyone fill out reports to detail their complaints. It turned out that the number one complaint was they had to fill out too many reports. So I spent the day preparing a report for my boss, explaining that the team was tired of filling out reports. That was what I did all day before I found the boogers. Not all of the boogers were dry, a few wet ones got stuck to my new pants, that is how I first discovered them. I kneeled down to investigate and found a collage of slime and mucus covering my front door. I also heard a machine-like rumbling noise under my house. Anyway, I was not too bothered by the boogers on the door. I decided to clean them off the door after I checked out the rumbling noise. I hoped it all stopped at the door because we had just painted the walls and installed new floors. The boogers made me think of my kids, I mean, that is why I sit in traffic to work a terrible job for almost no pay five, sometimes six, days a week. What I needed was a hug. Every time I come home, my baby girl runs to the front door and gives me a great big starfish hug. It's the greatest feeling in the world, to be loved like that. I'm telling you, Danny, having kids changes everything. I remember holding Tyler when he was born. Before that moment, I was like you, sort of, in that I did not have kids. I had time for silly things like going to the movies, walking on the beach, and pursuing a career. But when I first held Tyler, everything changed. I can't describe it. It was a spiritual awakening that overwhelmed my soul. From that point on, my life had a singular purpose—to provide for my family. And Sophia's starfish hug made all the toil and pain worthwhile. I opened the front door and braced for the hug. Around the corner, I heard Lynn say, 'Daddy's home.' Then I heard those sweet little footsteps running down the hall. Neither one of us thought much about it at the time but we should have. See, Lynn and I had been taking shifts. We adjusted our working hours so we could stay home with Sophia. We could not afford childcare at home and preschool would not take her until she was potty trained. We had tried everything—giving her candy if she did number one in the potty, more candy for number two. None of it worked.

Then Lynn read about a method of last resort, where you let the child run around the house without any pants on. So Lynn tried it that morning. Well, in the excitement, Sophia peed all over the floor as she ran toward me. It went everywhere and she slipped on her pee and went airborne. The sudden horizontal flight pattern scared her into releasing a series of poop bombs, all of which exploded on our new floor and walls. Sophia skidded to a stop at my feet. Scared, but uninjured, she jumped up and hugged tightly to my new pants. She peered up at me with that pitiful look like she did not know what had happened and wondered if she did something wrong but did not know because she had only been on this planet for twenty-something months. I stood there in the doorway, having not yet taken one step into the house and there was a disaster zone already waiting for me. I wanted to help clean up the mess, but I was concerned about the noise under the house. When I crawled under the house, I found three inches of standing water and signs of wild animals living under there, so . . ."

"Stop!" Danny said. "That's enough. I can help. I know what happens next."

"You do? How?"

"Easy. That rumbling noise was just a trick. There was nothing to it. Like most things, it'll go away with time. But by trying to fix it, you found something else and then you found something else and then something else and you chased that house around all day and night like a dog that can't catch his tail. You should have just pretended you never heard the noise."

"What? I can't do that."

"Sure you can. Just pretend that you did not kneel down to check on those boogers. You would have never heard the noise if you just walked right into the house."

"That's ridiculous."

"No, it's genius. Same with the boogers. Just pretend you never saw them."

"But there will be boogers on my front door."

"Only for awhile. They will crust up and bugs will eat them. Just pretend you went through a different door."

"What about the poop?"

"I'm still thinking about that one. I don't have much experience with kids and poop. I, however, have a lifetime of experience in ignoring problems. Here is an example. Earlier this year, I decided to make some beer. Why? I don't know. I found out quickly that making beer is a lot of work and that it was cheaper to go to the store and buy beer. Halfway through the process, I gave up. I had gotten to the point where you ferment the beer. This is where you pour sugar and yeast into an already sugary liquid. When the yeast eats the sugar, it produces bubbles, lots of bubbles and carbonation. Well, I added the sugar and yeast to a very large glass container full of liquid, capped it off, and stored it in a closet. That was the end of it for me. I went on vacation and forgot about it. What do you think happened?"

"It exploded."

"Exactly. The pressure built up such that it burst like a huge bomb. Glass and syrupy liquid went everywhere. So what did I do about it?"

"Knowing you, you did nothing."

"Precisely, but not by choice. I was on vacation when it exploded and I did not find out about the explosion until six months had passed. By that time, the syrupy juice had soaked through the wooden floor and disappeared. Even the smell was faint. I vacuumed the glass shrapnel and was done with it. Took all of thirty seconds. What would you have done if you knew that bottle had exploded?"

"Worked diligently to clean up the mess and dry the floors and walls. I would probably repaint them, if not replace them entirely."

"But not if you were on vacation and did not know about it. Now, tell me about the dead squirrels."

"Ok. Later that same day, after the poop bomb, I sat down exhausted in my favorite chair, right next to the fireplace. We never use the fireplace because we live in Savannah, which has a four-day winter. A fly buzzed by. Then another. And another. And another. They were coming out of the fireplace by the dozens."

"Stop right there," Danny said. "At this point, you should have pretended you were on vacation."

"At my house?"

"No, anywhere but your house."

"Can't do that."

"Why not?"

"Because I am broke. Can't afford vacation. I decided to check it out and opened the fireplace doors. There were maggots everywhere, dripping from the chimney like rain. The stench was suffocating. I pulled seven dead squirrels out and the flies kept coming. There were more, many more. My chimney had apparently served as a high-rise condominium for the local squirrel population until it got too crowded and they clogged up the flue. I did what I could but gave up and called a professional chimney sweep. He wouldn't touch it. Two days later, I'm still scraping remnants of squirrel from the flue. That's when I found a large crack. I called the chimney sweep again and he got excited, says he can fix it for an easy ten thousand dollars. I became upset and offended and ran him off. He should have known I could not afford that type of repair. I channeled all of my rage and frustration into cleaning that chimney. It took all weekend, but I removed all the squirrels. The stench is still there, but I'm working on that too. It's on my list."

"I'm telling you, man, just pretend you're on vacation. Let nature and time help you out. They will clean that for you at no cost."

"Too late."

"There is another approach that usually works in this type of situation."

"What is that?"

"Set it on fire."

"Damn. I should have thought of that."

"Yeah, just pretend it is winter and build a roaring fire. It's a little bit of work, but you would have been done in an hour or less."

"Maybe next time," I said. "I better get back to work now. I'll see you at your place. I think Lynn and the kids are already there."

"Sounds good," Danny said. "See you there."

After work, I arrived at Danny's, exhausted from the week and looking forward to seeing my family. I needed that starfish hug. Lynn and Tyler were outside playing.

"Where's Sophia?" I asked.

"Inside," Lynn said. "Napping, but she needs to wake up now or she will be up all night."

"I will go check on her."

I walked in and the first thing I saw was Sophia. Her nose was running like a faucet as it often did. She looked at me and smiled, beaming with pride.

"Wook, Daddy," Sophia said. "Wook what I made for you!"

On Danny's recently painted walls, she had painted a sticky, snotty collage of little handprints.

"It is beautiful, sweetums," I said. "Now let's go clean your hands."

On our way to the sink, I found a large piece of furniture and pushed it in front of her little masterpiece.

I thought, I'll just pretend it never happened.

CHAPTER 22

## *Jesse's Watch*

J esse peered out one of the windows at the top of his house. He looked across the marsh for the dark boat. He had stopped diving after seeing the dark boat. It was too risky, he thought. It might already be too late.

The sun started to set when he saw them. There were three men now, all on the dark boat. He watched them travel toward the big hole, the one that had held so many fossils and teeth and pieces of ancient history. He saw them anchor, right as the last piece of the sun disappeared behind the marsh. He knew what they were after.

Damn, he thought. They know.

## CHAPTER 23

# A Ship with No Name

"This is the spot," Charcoal said as he dropped the anchor.

"Here?" Mori asked. "In the middle of the waterway?"

"Yes. That's why we are here at night. Below us is a deep, dark hole. For years, millions of years, the river and creeks have swept back and forth over this hole. I have found some like it before. But this one is different. The black water keeps people away—that and the sharks and the alligators and the current. It is impossible to dive mid-current. I am certain there is a ship resting on the bottom. And I am certain that it is a pirate ship. It is a ship with no name. The best pirates operated that way. They saw no use in leaving a trail for someone else to find their gold. Without a name, the ship gets lost in history. Not even legend can preserve it."

"So how do you know there is gold on it?" Mori asked.

"I don't. That is what we are going to find out tonight. There are dozens of ships—Spanish, French, and English—that wrecked from the Carolinas to Florida. Most of them have not been found. I found several of them, but the gold was gone. I told no one because it was no one else's business. On all the ships, there were signs of battle. Pirates sunk the ships, not storms. I am certain of this. The coast of Georgia is one of the few places untouched by man. It has always been that way. That is why pirates used it as a haven, but even the pirates could not find refuge here for long. The weather and bugs and animals did not allow it."

"I see," Mori said.

"I have the ship marked. We'll send the submersible down and see what is at the bottom."

Charcoal showed them the device. It included lights and cameras and other sensors.

"In addition to taking digital images," Charcoal said, "it can detect the presence of gold. It is one of a kind. I had it built for this very purpose. It is my secret weapon. It is one reason why I find sunken treasure better than anyone else."

Charcoal placed the device into the water and let it sink. Using a remote control, he navigated the device through the murky water. He had a screen displaying video as the submersible traveled through the water.

"There it is!" he said.

Mori and Judd looked at the screen. Sure enough, they saw a sunken ship. They could see the bow and the masts and everything that remained. The ship looked well preserved in the mud and darkness.

"Look at that ship!" Charcoal said with pride. "I knew it was here."

Charcoal navigated the device around the boat as if it were a child's toy. At first, he seemed ecstatic that he had once again found his ship, but after an hour of surveying the ship, his mood changed.

"Bad news, guys," Charcoal said.

"What do you mean?" Mori asked.

"The ship is there all right, but I am not picking up signs of any gold."

"Could it be buried below it? In the mud?" Mori asked.

"I doubt it. This device is usually spot on."

"Damn," Mori said.

Charcoal brought the device back to the surface and put it on the boat.

"Let's go back," he said. "There is nothing else we can do tonight and we do not want to draw attention to ourselves. A few months ago, I saw another boat here, some crazy old man was fishing or something."

"What old man?" Mori asked.

"I don't know, but he was no treasure hunter. I can promise you that. Maybe you know him."

"Describe him to me," Mori said.

"He's probably about seventy years old and has a sailboat. I think he lives on one of these islands, but I'm not sure."

"I'll check him out," Mori said.

"Sounds good. Let me know what you find out. Let's meet again in a month. The tide should be slack by then. I will dive to the bottom and see if I can find something the submersible missed. But I'll need a slack tide. It is too dangerous otherwise."

"Ok," Mori said.

"Sorry, guys," Charcoal said. "I appreciate what you have done so far. Let's not give up yet."

## CHAPTER 24

# *The Dance*

"Wing-a-wound the wosies!
A pocket fuhl of posies!
Ashes! Ashes!
We all fall down!"

The song sounded so much sweeter when sung by a child.

"Do it again, Daddy!" Sophia said.

Sophia, Tyler, and I stood up, held hands, and danced around again while Sophia sang. It was our fortieth iteration.

"Wing-a-wound the wosies!
A pocket fuhl of posies!
Ashes! Ashes!

We all fall down."

"Do it again, Daddy!" Sophia said.

"That's enough, sweetums," I said, sitting down exhausted. "We can't do this forever."

"Daddy, just one more time."

"No, sweetums. There is always just one more time. We'll do it another day."

"Ok."

Six months pregnant and showing, Lynn walked in with a large binder and a notebook.

"All right, kids, go play somewhere else. I need your daddy to help me with something."

"Uh," I said. "We were just playing ring-a-round the rosies. Can we just do it one more time?"

"No. You can do it another day."

"Ok."

Lynn sat down beside me with her arsenal of paperwork.

"We are going to name our child today," she said.

"Name our child? You mean, like a nickname? I think Tyler and Sophia sound fine."

"No. I'm talking about this child," she said, pointing to her stomach.

"Oh yeah, that one," I said. "It is easy to forget that there is another human being living inside of you, isn't it?"

"No, it is not. This baby needs a name and we are going to give her a name today. There are a thousand things we need to do before she arrives and we need her name to do most of them."

"I don't know," I said. "We still have three months to think about this and I don't see any reason to rush it. Don't you think we should keep our options open until she is born?"

"No. We are not doing that again. I let you drag your feet with Tyler and you remember what happened with him."

"Not really."

"Three days after he was born, he still did not have a name! All of his medical records were filed under 'Baby Boy Scott.' Fortunately, the hospital kicked us out of the maternity ward, forcing us to sign all the birth certificate paperwork."

"I remember now, we were deadlocked in a negotiation."

"It was not and is not a negotiation! It is the child's permanent name!"

"I wanted to name him Hugh, you know, after my father and my grandfather."

"Because we waited so long, it is no surprise that they screwed up the paperwork. They were probably trying to rush it through," Lynn said.

"Maybe, but we were stationed overseas at the time," I said. "I think the Italians were just confused."

"They misspelled his name!"

"True, but all the nurses thought it was so cute."

"It is not healthy for a boy to have 'Hug' as his middle name. Think about middle school."

"Maybe we can change it later. I don't even know where to start with changing a child's name with a birth certificate from Sicily," I said. "All right. All right. We will do it your way this time."

"Thank you."

"What name do you have in mind?" I asked.

"I have narrowed down the list to one hundred and thirty-seven acceptable names. Here is the spreadsheet. This is your copy. I have another."

"Ok."

"I organized the list based on the popularity of the name. The most popular names are at the top, with the other names listed in descending order according to their popularity. I eliminated the most popular and least popular names. I want our daughter to have a unique name, but not too unique."

"Ok."

"Now, from this list we can take several approaches, but there are rules."

"Ok."

"No names of past girlfriends."

"And?"

"Well, that's it. That is the only rule."

"Ok."

"As for the approaches to naming our daughter, we could look at family names or biblical names."

"I don't really know any girl names from the Bible, except Mary."

"You are worthless, but that is not important. We will put biblical names and family names to the side for now. Let's start in the middle of my list and work our way down."

"That sounds good. We'll know the right name when we hear it. We will be able to feel it," I said.

"Don't be silly," Lynn said. "We are going to follow a process. We will analyze each name by listing the pros and cons of the name. Then we will list the pros and cons of the abbreviation. We do not want her embroidered backpack to be a target for teasing."

"How about putting all of this data aside and listening to our gut instinct?"

"No. It took me three days to compile this data. We are trusting the data, not your instinct."

"Ancient Native Americans had a good approach."

"What was that?"

"I think they would walk outside and name their child after the first animal they saw."

"We are not doing that."

"Why not? There could be something wonderful outside waiting for us, like a floating hummingbird or a peaceful dove or something I don't even know about. It's worth a shot, at least for inspiration."

"No. It is not. Not in our backyard. There is a higher probability that you will see a blind armadillo or a hungry squirrel or a lazy opossum. Let's get back to my list."

"Ok, but what about picking four or five names and then letting our daughter choose her first name when she is able to do so?"

"Maybe, I like the idea of letting her choose, but I would rather pick one name now. There is too much uncertainty in having multiple names, especially when you consider all the nursery decorations we must put together before she arrives."

"Sure. Of course. The decorations. You and your mom are doing that, right?"

"Yes."

Lynn leaned back and put her binders to the side.

"I am so tired," she said. "And there is so much to do. It will be very different with three children."

"I know."

"It was so wonderful when we were stationed in Sicily, when we had Rosa to help us with our one child."

"I miss Sicily," I said.

"It was a great place to have a baby," Lynn said.

"They loved babies in Sicily," I said.

"I loved Rosa," Lynn said.

"Rosa was a wonderful person. And it was so nice to have enough money to pay someone to help watch Tyler at home."

"I wish we could have done more for Rosa. She had such a kind and loving soul. Remember how she always brought a piece of chocolate in her pocketbook?"

"Yes."

"Tyler loved that chocolate."

"He loved Rosa," I said.

"Remember how he cried when we said goodbye to Rosa, the day before we left Sicily," Lynn said.

"Yes."

"He was so young. I don't know how he knew we were leaving for good. But he knew."

"Yes. He knew," I said, putting one arm around Lynn and the other on her stomach.

"I wish we could have brought Rosa here with us," Lynn said.

"Did you feel that?" I said.

"Yes," Lynn said, laughing.

"She's kicking!"

"No, I think she's dancing. It tickles."

"Do you think she can hear us?"

"Of course she can hear us."

I leaned closer to Lynn's stomach.

"Hello, little baby girl," I said. "We can't wait to meet you. Maybe someday we can take you to Sicily, where you can meet Rosa."

"She kicked again!" Lynn said. "Say her name again."

"Who? Rosa?"

"She's dancing now. She loves it."

We both looked at each other and smiled. It was perfect. I leaned even closer to Lynn's stomach.

"Hello, Baby Rosa," I said. "Daddy loves you."

## CHAPTER 25

# *Baby Rosa*

Alarge storm rolled in, knocking out our power and phones. I went from room to room checking on everyone. When I got to our room, I knew something was wrong. Lynn lay on the bed holding her stomach.

"I'm having contractions," she said.

"Let's go," I said. "We don't have time to wait for an ambulance."

When Tyler was born, he came fast. Sophia came even faster. I knew enough to know we needed to hurry. At six months, it was too early.

I ran outside to find a neighbor who could watch Tyler and Sophia. Bolting out my front door, I saw Pastor David and his wife walking down the road.

"I need help," I said.

"Lynn is having contractions. She's only six months. Can you please watch our children?"

"Yes," Pastor David's wife said.

"They are inside. I need to go now and cannot wait on an ambulance."

"I got it," she said.

The closest hospital was forty-five minutes away. We arrived in twenty-five minutes and I rushed Lynn to the ER.

"She is having contractions," I told the nurse. "She is only six months along. We have had two children and this is our third. She will be born any second."

I looked around and saw the waiting room full of people sick and in pain. But I knew we could not wait. There was not enough time.

"Come with me," the nurse said, taking us back to a room to measure Lynn's vitals. A doctor rushed in and also looked at Lynn's vitals.

"Has your blood pressure ever been this high?" the doctor asked.

"Yes," Lynn said. "Twice, during labor with my other two children."

Her blood pressure had reached near stroke levels during all her labors. We knew there was little the doctor could do to reduce it. The doctor placed his stethoscope on Lynn's chest, listening to her heartbeat. Then he moved it to her stomach. Then back to her chest. Then back to her stomach.

"Doctor, how is the baby?" I asked. "How is the baby doing?"

He looked at me and listened again to Lynn's stomach and to her chest.

"Doctor, how is the baby? How is the baby's heartbeat?" I asked.

He stood up and let his stethoscope drop.

"I am so sorry," he said.

We both knew what that meant, but we could not believe it. It could not end this way.

"I am so sorry," he said. "We need to take you to the maternity ward, right now."

Nurses rushed in and wheeled Lynn away upstairs. It was a blur and a fog. The day before, Baby Rosa had been kicking and dancing in celebration of her new name. The day before, everything seemed perfect. Baby Rosa was perfect. The day before, I had dreamed of Baby Rosa in our backyard, chasing after Tyler and Sophia. The day before, I had dreamed of our three children throwing balls and building tree houses and dancing and putting on plays and growing up together. The day before, I had dreamed of Baby Rosa running to the door to meet her daddy with a great big starfish hug. The day before, it had all been so perfect and so right.

There was no time to cry. There was no time to reflect. Lynn was in danger. Everything moved so fast. There was so much to do. I stood beside Lynn in shock and awe of her strength. Baby Rosa is dead! I stood beside her in shock and awe of her steadiness as she endured the pains of labor. Baby Rosa is dead! I stood beside her in shock and awe of how she could endure those pains knowing that our baby girl's heart had stopped beating. I stood beside her in shock and awe, unable to comprehend that our baby girl was dead inside my wife's body. Baby Rosa is dead!

How could any of this be real?

Baby Rosa arrived still, her eyes shut, forever asleep.

The doctors and nurses left us alone. It ended as suddenly as it had begun. I held my wife and hugged her and we cried. Baby Rosa was gone. I wanted so much to have been Baby Rosa's father. I wanted to play when she wanted to play. I wanted to dance when she wanted to dance. I wanted to be there when she wanted me to be there.

How could it end this way?

I held my wife and we cried until we could cry no more. Exhaustion set in, allowing sweet sleep to blanket our pain. That night, I dreamed a powerful dream, full of memories of our first days with Tyler and Sophia, but my dreams of starfish hugs from Baby Rosa faded away.

# PART THREE

CHAPTER 26

## *Moving On*

The next morning, a grief counselor visited us in the hospital room. Neither Lynn nor I knew how to grieve. The counselor explained that there were five stages in the grief process. First—denial and isolation. Second—anger. Third—guilt. Fourth—depression. Fifth and finally—acceptance.

"Not everyone gets to the final stage," she said. "But it is a gift if you do make it there. The process takes time. I suggest that you set aside time to grieve."

"Thank you," I said as we packed up to leave the hospital.

We did not make it to the first stage.

We returned home and found out Tyler had the flu. And I had to go to work the next day.

"I need to miss work for a week," I told my boss.

"Why?" he asked.

"The flu."

"You look fine to me."

"I'm fine now. But I will need to call in sick in about nine days. I will be out with the flu."

"I don't understand," he said.

"Do you have children?" I asked.

"No."

"My son is sick with the flu and my wife is taking care of him, so my wife will get the flu in about three days. In another three days, my daughter will get the flu. Then I will get it three days later. This is the best-case scenario."

"Ok."

"At least we have time to plan for it," I said.

It turned out I was wrong. Less than two days after Tyler got the flu, it struck our entire family at the same time. For more than a week, the four of us took turns vomiting and passing out in between bouts of diarrhea. At the peak of our misery, I slipped and fell in the bathroom, at least, that is what I thought had happened. There were no witnesses to the event and I lost all memory of it. Lynn said she heard a loud crash in the bathroom and crawled over to see what had happened. Realizing that I was either dead or about to die from loss of blood, she mustered all of her energy to call 911. Exhausted from her own efforts, she passed out.

When I came to, a first responder was standing over me. I was on the floor in my bathroom, semi-conscious in a pool of my own blood.

"Oh shit!" said the first responder. "Leroy, come look at this!"

I heard Leroy's footsteps.

"Oh shit!" Leroy said.

They both stood there looking at me as if I were a dead circus freak.

"Come on, guys!" I mumbled. "It can't be that bad. I mean, you drive an ambulance for a living."

"He ain't dead!" Leroy said.

"I'll get the stretcher," the other man said.

"Sorry, man," Leroy said. "I've seen a lot of bad stuff. But this here . . ."

"Just stop! That's enough," I said.

"You got it, man. Sorry, I ain't used to seeing that much blood," Leroy said. "The stretcher is coming. We're going to get you to the hospital real fast."

"Stretcher?" I said, trying to sit up. "First, I need five minutes to myself in here."

"No, sir. We need to put you on the stretcher now," Leroy said.

"Well, do that after I'm finished. I need five minutes to myself before we go."

"You are hurt pretty bad, man. I think we should go now."

"Five minutes!" I said. "I need five minutes to sit on the toilet before we go. Do you understand!"

"Oh. I see what you're saying, man," Leroy said. "Let me just say this. You is one tough dude. See, when I saw you, I figured you had been murdered and your wife was passed out in the hallway. Then there was the kids. They was just . . ."

"Please, just close the door and give me five minutes!"

"You got it, man."

To close the gaping wound, the surgeon used thirty-seven staples and hundreds of stitches running from the top of my skull down to my neck. It looked like he had pinned a foot-long caterpillar to my head.

"It seems a little loose," I told the surgeon, wondering if Tyler could have done a better job.

"I did that on purpose. You never know when you might need to open it back up. It is kind of like a zipper," he said proudly.

"Open it back up?" I asked, looking to see if the surgeon had any thumbs.

"You know, if it gets dirt in it or something."

"Can't you just close it so no dirt gets in?"

"Yes, but I prefer this approach. It gives us more options if there is an infection, especially with you having the flu right now."

"Ok."

A few days later, our family crawled out from our flu misery and we went back to our routine, which meant I went back to work.

"I'm sorry, Mel," my boss said, trying not to stare at the puss and blood oozing from my head and neck. "It is just hard not to stare."

"I know," I said.

"Try to look at me straight ahead," he said.

I turned.

"Yes, that's better," he said. "But it is going to be a distraction for the team, especially with our open-style office."

"I know, but what can I do?" I asked.

"You could use the spare office for a few days. Keep the door shut and I'll tell everyone just to talk to you through the door."

"Sounds good."

"Let's see," he said, looking at his calendar. "Ah! This is great. We volunteered to send someone to the local high school to speak to a class at career day tomorrow. Perfect! This will get you out of the office for a day. Maybe some of the blood and puss will crust up by the time you get back."

"Ok," I said. "Sounds like a good plan."

At career day, there were three of us speaking to the class. A police officer. A firefighter. And me.

I eased into the room so that the back of my head faced away from the students. I found a chair at the front near the other speakers and waited my turn, careful not to reveal the mess running down the back of my head and neck.

The police officer went first.

"Hi, class," he said. "I am a police officer. It is my job to keep the community safe and to make sure that our citizens follow the law and . . ."

"Have you ever shot a person?" one of the students asked.

"No," he replied. "Not on purpose. As I was saying, it is very important to follow the law and . . ."

"How fast can your car go?" another student asked.

"Very fast, but I only drive the speed limit unless I am chasing someone because . . ."

"Is that a real gun?" another asked.

The students peppered the officer with questions about guns and cars and drugs and a bunch of other stuff that they found incredibly interesting. When the police officer's time was up, he explained that he also had a second job as a security officer so he could make enough money to feed his family and pay his bills.

The firefighter's presentation proceeded in the same way, starting with an engaging dialogue on fires and trucks and then ended with a plug for his second job as a member of a landscaping crew. The firefighter explained that he took the second job because he needed money to feed his family and pay his bills.

So far, the students had found the discussion exciting and interesting, except the part about not making any money.

It was my turn. I was torn between describing my job as a rewarding, profitable career and telling the truth.

"Hello, students," I said, standing as far away as possible from them. "My name is Melvin Scott and I am a middle manager at a large corporation . . ."

"So, what is your second job?" a student asked.

"Um. Well, I don't really have time for a second job because . . ."

"Oh my God! There's something crawling on his head!" another student screamed.

"Oh, it's nothing," I said, spinning around so they could see that there was no need for alarm.

"Quick! Someone kill it!" another student yelled.

"It's chewing on his neck!" another screamed.

"No. No. No. Please sit down," I said. "That's just a bit of blood oozing from my wound. I had an accident recently. It's ok."

Some of the students sat back in their desks.

Feeling faint, I found a chair in the middle of the classroom and sat down.

"So, what happened?" a student asked, mistaking my decision to rest as a cue that I wanted to tell them the whole story.

"So, what happened?" the student asked again.

"It's not important," I said.

"Come on, tell us," the mob replied.

So I told them.

"One of my children got sick at school so I had to get some staples in my head."

Blank stares and silence filled the room. I wanted to talk about anything else, but it was clear they would not allow that to happen. Maybe it was the loss of blood or maybe it was the painkillers or maybe it was my complete lapse of judgment that influenced my bad decision. I figured, what the hell, they deserved the truth.

"Like I said earlier, I am a middle manager at a large corporation. My job mostly involves sifting through daily reports from my team so I can compile a daily report for my boss. It is a terrible job and does not pay well, but I do it so I can feed my family and pay our bills. As a dad, it is my main job to help keep two small human beings alive. A dad should also provide loving guidance, discipline, and encouragement, but I don't have much time for that because I am usually either working or commuting to work. About two weeks ago, one of my children got the flu along with some other third-world virus, we think, because he suffered from serious diarrhea, vomiting, and hallucinations. Within two days, my entire family was sick. My wife and I took turns bringing bread and water to each other and our children. This kept us alive during the worst of it. Then I fell in the bathroom. Fortunately, the impact from the fall knocked me out and I don't remember what happened, but I suspect I slipped on my own vomit. During the fall, I hit my head and neck on something, which is why I have this large gash running down the back of my head and neck. The next thing I remember is an ambulance driver standing over me. He looked at me and said, 'Oh shit!' Let this be a lesson to any of you future ambulance drivers—do not use that type of language when rescuing someone, even if you think they are dead. They wanted to take me to the hospital, but I knew diarrhea was about to set in, so I . . ."

"All right, class," the teacher said. "Unfortunately, Mr. Scott's time is up. Let's, uh, thank Mr. Scott for his presentation."

Complete silence.

Then one pale kid in the back vomited on himself.

"Um. Thank you, Mr. Scott, that was, uh, very vivid of you to share with us the challenges you face as a manager and a father."

I nodded and walked toward the door. I was groggy and a little disappointed that I could not teach the students anything useful. As I was leaving, the teacher quickly transitioned to the next subject.

"And now, class, we will be discussing sex education," the teacher said. "I think we all now understand why the best approach to birth control is abstinence . . ."

Well. Maybe I taught them something, even if they did not get to hear all the details.

CHAPTER 27

## *A Golden Coin*

Pastor David's wife stopped by our house concerned, about us and about Pastor David.

"Please just let me know if there is anything I can
do," she said.

"Thank you, but we are doing better now," I said. "You
have already done too much. We appreciate you watching
our kids that night. How is Pastor David doing?"

"Ok, I guess," she said.

"You know, he is welcome here anytime," I said.

"Thank you, Mel. You have been so kind to him," she
said. "He was not always this way."

"I know. I remember. What happened?"

"I don't know," she said, "but I remember the day it
happened."

"On Easter, at church, right?"

"No. That is what everyone thinks."

I stood silent.

"I have not told anyone this, but I think I need to now," she said. "I have not told anyone because I did not think anyone would believe me. During the week before Easter, we went to River Street. It was my idea and I have regretted it ever since. There was a craft show and we stopped at a strange booth. I don't know how to describe it any other way, but the lady at the booth was a witch of some sort. She had a sign that said, 'Devil's Friend.' Out of curiosity, we stopped to talk to her. She put him under a trance of some kind. It was like hypnotism, but something else. I thought he was having a stroke. He has not been the same since."

"Odd," I said.

"And he keeps going back. I don't know what to do. He spends a lot of time with the witch lady and her crazy boyfriend—some old man who sells bones and shark teeth. I would ask him to stop going to River Street, but he wouldn't listen. And besides, he always brings back one of these."

She showed me a gold coin. I recognized the coin from somewhere. It was marked with a spear piercing a heart.

"It is all so dark and sad," she said. "I don't know what to do, but we need the money because we stopped accepting money from the church because he never goes to church anymore. We get by from pawning these coins each week."

I could tell she was upset.

"It's ok," I said. "I believe you. And I have seen that coin before. At the right time, I will try to talk to Pastor David about it."

"Thank you."

"And don't worry," I said. "I will keep this between you and me."

"Thank you."

CHAPTER 28

# *The Storm*

I loved my wife and I knew she loved me but we did not often express our love so much in words. But there were three words that, when spoken at the right time, could touch one's soul. There was magic in those three words—magic that transcends human understanding. Maybe that is why I felt so moved when she said those three words to me. Whatever the reason or cause, I did not know how much I needed to hear those three words until I heard them that morning. Understanding the deep needs of her husband, my wife held my hands, looked into my eyes, and said, "Please, go fishing."

"Say that again?" I said.

"Please, go fishing," she said.

"Are you feeling ok?" I asked. "Do you need some aspirin or maybe a sedative or maybe the opposite of a sedative?"

"No."

"Maybe you are on some type of medication I don't know about?"

"No," she said. "I think it would be good for you to take some time off and go fishing."

"I don't know if I should do that," I said, rummaging around a closet for my tackle box. "I don't have any vacation time at work, but there is a little pond nearby, maybe I could go there this afternoon for a few hours."

"I think you should invite Maksim and Dice over and spend a weekend fishing with them."

"You mean, like a real fishing trip?" I asked.

"Yes."

"With Maks and Dice? From college?"

"Yes."

"Honey, I really don't think you are thinking straight," I said. "Maybe we should get this in writing first."

"No, I'm fine. Stop being such an idiot and just plan a fishing trip. Call your friends and tell them to come down for a weekend."

"You really want me to call the Wild Weasel and Silent Maks?"

"Yes, but I thought Maks's nickname in college was the Black Cat, on account of his bad luck."

"It was. We called him a lot of things, but I like Silent Maks the best."

Maks had earned the nickname Black Cat by his own rite. Bad luck followed him like the plague, and anyone who saw Maks knew it was near. There were countless tales, all true, of how Maks screwed up something or injured someone or hurt himself, despite the likelihood of injury or failure being a statistical impossibility. But he always had good intentions. That might have been part of the problem.

Take this one instance as an illustration. In college, the three of us volunteered to participate in a softball game as a fundraiser for sick children in the community. Perhaps we did so to atone for that week's sins. I do not remember. And I do not remember the outcome of that game. I remember one and only one moment from that day. It was Maks's turn to bat. He stepped up to the plate and got in his stance as if nothing incredibly bad was about to happen. As the pitch slowly approached Maks, he took a mighty swing at the ball. He put all of his energy and strength into that swing. Of course, he missed. A big whiff. There was nothing malicious or unusual about his swing except that the bat flew out of his hands and over a high fence. The bat screamed through the air in what seemed like slow motion. It struck an old man in the face, ricocheted off the old man, and then hit an infant in the head. We all felt terrible for the old man and for the infant and for Maks. To most everyone in attendance, the string of events seemed to be a complete accident. And it was an accident in the sense that Maks had no intent to injure anyone. But those who knew the history of Maks's bad luck, knew it was no accident.

Despite his extreme bad luck, nothing fazed Maks. This can only be explained by his unparalleled stoicism. I did not know many Russians. Only one—Maks. So maybe there are other human beings on this planet who possess the same ability to remain calm and steady during any circumstance. Maks's family left Russia for America when he was about twelve. They landed in New Jersey. So when I first met Maks, he was part Russian and part New Jerseyan, but mostly Russian.

I remember introducing Maks to Dice. We were all in a business-law class together.

"Dice, this is my friend Maks. He's from Russia."

"I'm not from Russia," Maks said. "I'm from the Ukraine."

"Same thing," I said. "Anyway, Maks, this is Dice. He is from the Ozark Mountains in Oklahoma."

"Arkansas," Dice said. "Nice to meet you, Maks."

The three of us became fast friends due, I think, to the fact that we did not share the study habits of our fellow students.

"These people are crazy," Dice said. "I mean, they study all the time. I can't believe that we are halfway through the semester and not one person has been caught unprepared."

"It's amazing," I said. "It is a good thing the professor has not called on me. I try to keep up, but I bet I don't know half of the cases on any given day."

"It's just too much," Dice said.

In our business-law class, the professor used the socratic method, which resembled the approach in actual law school, I think. From what I could tell, it was the easiest job on the planet for a teacher. All he had to do was ask students to tell him about such-and-such case. It was, however, a nightmare for students.

Each day in class, the professor selected at random a student to brief each case while the students sat in fear of being called on. Throughout the semester, the sense of fear grew and grew as each student successfully briefed the class on a case. No one wanted to be the first person to get caught unprepared. Even Dice and I upped our study habits as the semester continued.

Not Maks. No fear in life—real or imaginary—could alter his study habits. No amount of pressure could force him to prepare for class.

I remember the day the inevitable happened. Maks, as usual, remained still and calm and cool in his chair as the professor picked away at all the other students sweating away in their seats. Then it happened—the professor called on Maksim Grandonev.

"Mr. Grandonev, please brief the class on *Pierson v. Post*," the professor said.

It was an easy case to brief. It had something to do with the property rights of a wild animal. It was about a hunter who had killed a fox that was pursued by another hunter. The issue was about who owned the dead fox. A true American dispute, the case was important enough to make it all the way up to the Supreme Court of New York and became the most famous property case in American legal history. That is what our textbook taught us anyway.

Maks had never heard of it.

"Mr. Grandonev, please brief the class on *Pierson v. Post*."

Maks, in true stoic fashion, did not blink. He sat in complete silence.

"Mr. Grandonev, *Pierson v. Post*, please."

At first, the other students, including myself, were horrified. Our shared nightmare was playing out in living color with Maks. We pitied Maks. We felt for Maks as he sat there in silence. But for the Grace of God, there goes I, each of us thought. There was something different, however, with Maks. He was different.

"Mr. Grandonev?" the professor continued.

Maks continued to stare at the professor in a stunning display of absolutely no emotion.

"Mr. Grandonev?" the professor said.

Maks calmly looked down at his book and then back at the professor. His expression never changed. He never said, "I don't know" or "I'm not sure" or "I'm sorry I did not prepare today" or anything else that a normal human being would say. He just sat there in complete silence, showing no emotion.

"Mr. Grandonev?"

We all soon realized that Maks would not break. Nothing in this world could break his silence. Caught off guard, the professor did not know how to respond. No one dared laugh or utter a word or make a sound that might interrupt the beautiful silence. In it, we somehow found peace and freedom. It was ok to be unprepared. It was ok to be a mere student. Life would go on.

"Ms. Hernandez," the professor said. "Can you please brief the class on *Pierson v. Post*?"

Maks had won. Through his steady genius, the silent treatment was born. But to this day I know no other who can execute it as perfectly as Maks.

I do not know why we called Dice the Wild Weasel and I do not think he liked it. He was loyal and trustworthy in character and exactly the opposite of a weasel. He did have long toes and liked to climb things when he was drinking, despite his extreme fear of heights, but I am pretty sure none of these traits resemble a weasel either. For whatever reason, we called him the Wild Weasel, a name that became more permanent and lasting to us than any given or legal name. It was simply one of those things out of Dice's control.

Maks and Dice were both stalwart friends of mine. They were the best kind of friends. They were the kind of friends that you did not feel the need to call or e-mail or text at all. After twenty years of zero communication, we met during a chance meeting and found that our bond of friendship had grown even stronger. Our friendship rested on the kind of loyalty that knows no reason. It was this shared virtue of loyalty, perhaps, that doomed most of our adventures. It was either that or Maks's bad luck.

A perfect storm had been building and I should have recognized all the signs leading up to the disaster. Lynn had just given me the go-ahead to plan a big fishing trip. That was fair warning enough. Add this to the fact that, a few days earlier, I had met up with Dice and Maks for lunch in Savannah after not seeing them for twenty years. At the lunch, they suggested we meet up soon for a weekend. I should have known this was all too good to be true.

Nothing good ever happened when I met up with friends from college, probably because our mindsets immediately reset to the levels of stupidity and recklessness we knew in college. Our aging bodies, however, could no longer cope with the consequences stemming from thinking that one is eighteen years old and invincible.

"It seems like it was just yesterday when we were in college together," Dice had said at lunch.

He was right. Again, that was the problem. While our brains united to rejoice in the celebration of and potential for jackassary, the rest of my body winced. Just the prospect of meeting up with the Wild Weasel and Silent Maks caused my liver to twitch.

Maks and Dice worked for different companies in different parts of America. Business had brought them to Savannah during the same week, giving us the opportunity to rekindle our friendship. To my great surprise, both Maks and Dice had become very successful in their careers.

"How did you do it?" I asked.

"Well," Dice said, "I worked about sixty hours a week, every week, for ten years on top of a two hour commute, one way, until I finally got promoted."

"Same here," Maks said.

"Once I got promoted, I worked even more," Dice said.

"Same here," Maks said.

"What about your kids and family? How are they doing?" I asked.

"The family is doing fine, but I don't ever see them," Dice said. "I leave when they are asleep and return home when they are asleep. Sometimes, when I am not traveling, I get to see them on the weekend, but they are usually with a friend. It is better this way, I think. I don't know what we would do if I did have time to see them."

"Same here," said Maks.

"What about you?" Dice asked.

"I'm doing ok, I guess. I used to be gone all the time, too, deployed with the service. So we moved down here to a house out in the woods near the marsh where I hoped to spend more time with my kids and maybe take them fishing or hunting once in a while. Now, I have a big house and a new van and a lot of debt and I'm pretty much broke, but I have a job and so does Lynn."

"Sounds like you are living the American Dream," Dice said.

"I guess so," I said.

"That sounds awesome," Dice said. "I live in a suburb surrounded by suburbs. I don't think I've been fishing in twenty years."

"Same here," said Maks.

"I got an idea," Dice said. "Let's plan a guys trip. Maks and I will fly down here and stay at your place. We'll set aside a couple of days to go fishing."

"Sounds good," Maks said.

"I can't wait to get out on a boat," Dice said.

"What do you want to fish for?" I asked.

"Doesn't matter," Dice said. "I'm game for anything. Let's try to catch something big."

"Sure," I said. "I'll talk to Lynn and we'll make it happen."

Little did I know that talking to Lynn would be so easy—one of the first signs.

Wasting no time in capitalizing on my wife's temporary lapse of sanity, I called Maks and Dice. They booked their flights. We were going fishing. We were going big.

Offshore fishing is unlike any other kind of fishing. It is the kind of fishing where a man can catch a fish that is bigger than the man. To offshore fish well from Georgia one should have a large, deep boat with two engines. That way, if one engine fails, there is a backup. This can save lives. The Gulf Stream runs parallel to the coast, about seventy-five miles from shore. In the fall, the inshore water is brown and cold. It turns green and cold on the way to the Gulf Stream. But in the Gulf Stream, the water is a deep royal blue and always warm. In the Gulf Stream, one can find tuna and mahi mahi and wahoo and billfish and sharks and countless other large animals that one can only find elsewhere in books. In the Gulf Stream, waves can grow large and steep with little notice. In the Gulf Stream, the weather can turn bad in an instant. These are just a few of the reasons why one should fish from a large, deep boat.

I had many reasons for not taking Dad's boat offshore—my kids and my wife and my kids. These were good reasons. But I had not yet taken Dad's boat offshore mostly because it was not a large, deep boat. It was a small skiff with one small engine. But that was ok because I was going fishing with Dice and Maks. They were grown men and loyal friends. They were ready for anything and, most importantly, they knew nothing about offshore fishing.

"You sure we should go that far offshore?" Dice asked, leaning on Dad's boat.

"Yes. That is where the fish are. The big ones," I said.

"When does the boat get here?" Dice asked.

"You're leaning on it," I said.

"Oh. I thought we were chartering a captain," he said.

"I am the captain," I said. "Hiring a professional would make it too easy and take all the adventure out of it."

"All right, I guess," Dice said. "I just figured we should take a bigger boat. This one only has one small seat."

"We will be standing most of the time anyway," I said, "especially if we are catching fish. There's no need for a bunch of seats, and, besides, I brought plenty of five-gallon buckets."

"I wondered what all of the buckets were for," he said.

"I don't need a bucket," Maks said. "I'll just stand."

"You might need one," I said. "A five-gallon bucket can serve as many things—a bait well, a fish box, an anchor well, a tackle box, a saltwater washdown, a head, and a lot of other things most big boats have. I save room this way, you see, by just taking a few five-gallon buckets."

"Ok, if you say so," Dice said. "What about this Bible? What is it doing here?"

"That's for Maks," I said.

"Maks, you don't believe in any of this stuff do you?" Dice asked.

"Nope," Maks said.

"That's what I thought," Dice said. "Communism doesn't allow for religion. In Russia, they're too focused on working hard and sharing everything, right Maks?"

"Yep," Maks said, "but I'm from the Ukraine."

"Whatever," Dice said. "Let's leave it here."

"I can't do that," I said. "I get superstitious on a boat, especially with Maks. I brought it to counter his bad luck, and, I figured, if I brought it, we wouldn't need it."

"Good point," Dice said. "Let's take it."

The three of us loaded into the skiff. With three of us in the boat, only a small amount of water lapped over the edges as we eased away from the marina, all of which was easily bailed out with a five-gallon bucket.

"Hold on," I said as I pushed the throttle forward. "Time to go fast!"

One advantage of having a small boat is you can go really fast, which was especially important during our trip because I knew the weather might turn bad around noon. Another advantage of a small boat is you can pull the plug out the back when going fast, allowing water to drain out so the crew can enjoy the ride instead of bailing water.

It was a perfect morning. We raced across the marsh through a fine mist of fog, smelling the sweet salty air. The sea looked like a never-ending sheet of glass. I took a sip of my coffee and watched the others standing on the bow of the boat as the sun began to rise. The sun burned off the fog and pushed a light breeze across the beam. In silence, we raced together across the golden rivers to the open sea.

The earthly paradise seemed so enchanting that time faded away. Hours seemed like minutes and minutes seemed like seconds. For a moment, time stood still.

"Why did you stop?" Dice asked. "Is everything ok?"

"I feel like I forgot something," I said.

"Really? We are filled to the brim. You have ice, right?" Dice asked.

"Yes."

"Beer?"

"Yes."

"Food?"

"Yes."

"Fishing rods?"

"Dammit."

I turned back and raced full throttle back to the marina, back to my house, back to the marina, and then we headed out again.

"How much time did we lose?" Dice asked.

"I don't know," I said. "I lost track of time, but we'll be all right, just a tighter window to catch fish. The weather usually picks up by noon."

We sped across the marsh and then past the barrier islands to the open sea again, still calm as far as one could see. Only the horizon lay before us. Faster and faster we sped across the water as the sea slowly turned from brown to green and then from green to blue. Soon, pods of dolphin danced in our wake, chasing brilliant schools of flying fish.

"We'll try here," I said, slowing the boat.

Except for the small hiccup with the fishing rods, nothing had gone wrong, which was a very unusual experience for me on a boat. Another sign.

We dropped our lines over live bottom, an underwater oasis, and immediately caught fish—two and three at a time. Seabass. Grouper. Snapper. And others. In less than thirty minutes, we had caught the limit on a rainbow of fish. We even landed an octopus that would not let go of a fish we had hooked. The fact that we had done so in a small skiff made it even sweeter. It was a perfect day.

"Let's troll for awhile," I said, bringing the boat to a comfortable speed of about five knots.

We trolled two lines behind us. Dice manned one. Maks the other.

"Fish on!" I yelled as line smoked off Maks's reel. I locked the drag and he fought the fish.

"Fish on!" I yelled and Dice fought another.

Behind the boat, two turquoise mahi mahi shot out of the water and into the sky, shaking and dancing through the air. Maks and Dice fought the fish for thirty minutes before getting them close enough to gaff.

Two fish in. Two lines back out.

"Fish on!" I yelled.

Maks and Dice had fought fish after fish and it seemed we could do so all day long. It was a perfect day.

"The guys back in the office will never believe this!" Dice yelled.

Maks nodded and smiled in one of his few displays of emotion. It was a perfect day.

It was about ten o'clock in the morning and the sea was still glass. I knew that if we left now, we would make it back by lunch, giving us time to clean all our fish.

"All right, guys. Lines in!" I said.

"What time is it?" Dice asked.

"Almost ten."

"We've only been out here a few hours," he said. "Let's just catch one more fish."

The words struck fear in my bones. This was the final sign. And I knew all too well that bad things happened after trying to do just one more of anything, especially when on a boat.

"I don't know, guys. I really think we should go in now. We have plenty already," I said.

"But the weather's perfect," Dice said. "Who knows when Maks and I will get a chance to do this again."

"I'm with Dice," Maks said. "Let's do it. Just one more fish."

"Ok. Just one more fish," I said.

It took about twenty minutes, just long enough for a deep sense of fear to set in for me. The wind picked up, but only enough to create a small chop in the waves. Maks and Dice remained unfazed in their ignorance, waiting for the line to race off the reel just one more time.

I had suffered through a countless number of catastrophes on a boat, all of which warned against trying just one more time. While we slowly trolled at sea, my mind drifted off to a time when my father and I were fishing in a creek near a barrier island in Charleston, South Carolina. We had not yet caught any fish that day but that was ok because we never caught fish anyway except stingrays and sharks. It was hot and the tide was falling. Dad wanted to throw the cast net to see if he could catch anything interesting. He kept throwing the cast net, catching baitfish, lots of useless baitfish. It was time to go home and leave the creek before the tide went too far out and left us stuck on a sandbar. I fished for redfish while he kept throwing the net. "Just one more time," he repeated. "Just one more cast." That's what he said right before we heard a loud snap and a high-pitched shrieking noise. The noise was Dad. "Dad, is everything ok?" I asked. His lips moved but made no sound because I had lost my hearing. I could tell by his grimacing that every-thing was not ok. Soon I could hear again. "Dad, what hap-pened?" I asked. "What snapped?" I checked the cast net. It was ok but my dad's bicep was now on top of his shoulder. "That's bad," I said. Then a redfish took my line, which was good because it helped us forget about his detached bicep. We lifted the anchor so we could chase the redfish. This was easy because the fish drug our little boat around the creek. Then the fish broke my line. "We should go," I said. "Just one more fish," I said and threw out my line. It was clear the heat was getting to Dad; he seemed to be drifting in and out of sleep. I had to keep splashing water on him to keep him awake. Hours passed. No more fish. We decided to go home. On our way back we found a boat stuck on a sandbar. An elderly man and his wife were in the water try-ing to push it off. "What happened?" I asked. "We were just trying to go around one more bend," the elderly man said. "Then we got stuck." I understood and helped push the boat but I could not do it alone. I went to our boat and splashed more water on Dad to wake him up. With Dad's help, I was able to confirm that we could not move the boat. "You can ride back with us," I said. "No, there's not much room in your boat," the elderly man said. "I think it is safer to wait here with my boat." I left them there with the sun setting on a falling tide. The tide would not bring enough water for at least seven hours. And that area was known to be thick with alligators and sharks. I thought it would be better to stay and persuade the man and his wife to go with us but I could not see them anymore because Dad had already driven the boat miles away. On the way back, we saw . . .

"Fish on!" Dice yelled.

The line raced off like we had never seen before. We all knew a monster had taken the bait.

"Watch the drag!" I yelled. "Loosen the drag! Too much! Tighten the drag! Too much! There you go, keep it there!"

Maks and Dice took turns fighting the beast. It was too big for one man to fight. They fought and fought that fish as we bobbed up and down on the waves. None of us noticed how big the waves had grown. An hour passed and they were still fighting the fish.

We saw the line start to rise.

"He's going to jump!" I yelled.

A large gray and white mass burst through the ocean's surface. He rose higher and higher, shaking his large head back and forth. In mid-flight, the giant shark paused and stared at all three of us in the eyes. He smiled, a wild smile, revealing his endless rows of jagged teeth. In one shake, he cut the line and dove back down into the sea.

We were about seventy miles offshore and could see storm clouds building, higher and higher, forming an anvil-shaped head.

"We need to go!" I said, pointing to the clouds.

They understood.

"Stay on the bow," I said. "We will need some weight up there when going over the waves."

The tall clouds formed a large dark mass. We headed west, racing against the storm, while the wind and seas picked up.

I had not seen another boat all day. We were alone.

The waves surged over seven feet, our boat still sixty miles from shore. Maks got sick and sent his breakfast over the side. Dice was not far behind. I had to slow the boat to about fifteen knots because I thought it might disintegrate against the waves. I tried to keep the bow into the waves and stay the course but it was hard to see with Dice and Maks bouncing up and down on the bow.

I pushed the throttle forward to ride up a large wave. Then I heard a loud metal clank. The boat lurched forward and then stopped.

"What was that?" Dice asked.

"The engine," I said.

"Did we hit something?"

"No, it's broken. It sounds like we blew a head."

I had no idea what had actually happened, except that the engine had made a loud clanky noise and then stopped. But I had heard many other fishermen speak of engines breaking at sea and this was normally referred to as blowing a head. I had a few extra spark plugs but did not bring any extra heads and would not know how to screw one back on anyway. I thought that telling them "we blew a head" instilled more confidence in them than "I think the engine made a loud clanky noise." As captain, I knew I must exude confidence, no matter what happened.

"Can you fix it?" Dice asked.

"Not in these seas," I said. "If I dropped the screws and washers we would be done for and, besides, we still have a little power. We're moving at two knots."

This was slower than the wind around us. Fortunately, the approaching storm was pushing us toward the shore.

"I'll call the Coast Guard and let them know our position," I said.

I turned the marine radio to channel 16, the emergency band.

"Mayday! Mayday! Mayday!" I said.

Dice and Maks looked at me in horror.

"It's just to get their attention," I said.

Silence.

"Mayday! Mayday! Mayday!" I said. No response. Finally, we reached a fishing boat near Savannah.

"This is Dirty Old Hookers," its captain responded. "We are anchored near Savannah and have received your signal. What is your position?"

I gave them my coordinates and waited.

"This is Dirty Old Hookers, the Coast Guard tower is down but we will relay your position. What's your situation?"

"We're sixty miles out. We blew a head."

"Are you under power?"

"Yes, we're traveling at about two knots."

"Roger that."

Through this exchange, I learned a valuable lesson about having your engine break at sea—never tell the truth. Had I told them we had no power instead of saying "yes, we're traveling at about two knots" the Coast Guard might have rescued us.

An hour passed.

"This is Dirty Old Hookers," the captain said over the radio. "The Coast Guard has instructed us to let you know they have informed BoatTow and that you are in BoatTow's jurisdiction. Right now, it is too rough and you are too far away for them to help. Radio back when you are twelve nautical miles out. Over."

What! I did the math. Sixty miles minus twelve miles at two knots equals . . . at this rate, twenty-four hours would pass before we reached help!

"What did they say?" Maks asked.

"Nothing important," I said. "We'll meet them between here and shore if need be."

I managed to keep the boat's bow into the waves, except when the storm spun us around like a top. Dice and Maks were doing better than expected. Dice was clinging to the side of the boat and Maks was passed out.

Then lightning started striking all around us. The water began to boil. Maks popped up and grabbed the Bible, leading Dice in prayer. During the madness, I tried to keep the boat pointed forward and remain calm. I stayed focused on keeping the boat heading in the right direction and in general I pretended that we were not all about to die. I knew that not letting the crew know we were all about to die is perhaps the most important role of the captain.

Maks came back to the helm. He said, "I think we are all about to die."

Then he noticed my empty fuel gauge.

"Mel," he said. "It looks like we are out of gas."

I had forgotten to tell Maks and Dice that all boats have faulty fuel gauges and that mine happened to break on empty.

Dice was now bailing out water with a five-gallon bucket.

"You don't need to worry about the gas," I said. "You should worry about the sharks circling us."

I am not exactly sure what triggered the sudden bout of diarrhea. Maybe it was my poor attempt at humor or maybe it was the fact that a school of large sharks was now circling us.

"Dice, quick! Throw Maks the five-gallon bucket!"

Aided by a slow and painful miracle, the winds picked up in our favor and pushed us back to shore, the return trip taking a little less than nineteen hours. We pulled the boat up to the marina and secured the bowline on a dock. Right before I turned the engine off, we ran out of gas.

We got off the boat and stood on the large bluff at the marina.

I looked at Dice and Maks and said, "Hell of a day, men. Welcome back to America."

Maks looked at me and yelled, "This is not America! Maybe it was America in some jacked-up time. This isn't even another country. This is another planet and that water is outer space. We just traveled seventy miles, almost to our grave, to catch a bleeping fish. There is an octopus in the boat and I think you plan on eating it. I live in America. America is a suburb full of rational human beings who don't risk their necks for a stupid fish. When they want fish, they go to the grocery store. This is crazy and you live in crazy land!"

"Dude!" I said.

"Maks is human!" Dice said.

Regaining his composure, Maks continued, "I don't know what got into me, guys. It was a good day. A hell of a day, but a good day."

"We should do it again sometime," Dice said.

"Anytime," I said.

"Next time, can we bring our kids?" Maks asked.

"No problem," I said.

It was good to see that our friendship and Silent Maks's reputation remained intact.

We left the boat and everything on it tied to the dock. Then we went back to my house. We needed sleep.

## CHAPTER 29

# *A Real Treasure*

Afew hours of sleep buried most of the bad memories from the day before. After we woke up, one part of the trip stood out most—we had caught fish, lots and lots of fish. We went back to the boat and found the fish still cool on ice.

"What a catch!" I said.

Not accustomed to actually catching fish, I was ill prepared to do anything with them. We found some spoons and a dull knife. In the heat of the day, we cleaned the fish until we ran out of beer. I found a cheap frying pan and cooked the catch. It might have been the best meal any of us had ever tasted.

Lynn walked outside to join us.

"How was your fishing trip?" she asked.

"Possibly the best fishing trip I've ever had," Dice said.

"Same here," Maks said.

"That's nice," she said. "I'm really glad you guys got to get out on the water and relax. I think Mel needed it. Mel, you remember that your family is coming over today and probably some of the neighbors too. It is Grandpapa's birthday."

"That's right," I said. "Thanks for reminding me."

I turned to Maks and Dice. "I forgot about Grandpapa's birthday. I thought we might get in another day of fishing, but we are running out of time. We could float around inshore for a few hours . . ."

"That's ok," Dice said. "A birthday party sounds good to me."

"Same here," Maks said.

"Ok," I said. "Grandpapa is one of a kind. He turns ninety-five today and he still plays eighteen holes of golf a day, three days a week."

"Wow!" Dice said.

"He hit a hole in one last year. He got a plaque and his name in the paper. I think he's pretty much a legend in his town."

Friends and family started arriving at our house. Even Dr. Manning showed up.

"Hello, Dr. Manning," I said. "Thank you for coming."

"Thank you for inviting me. I never want to miss a chance to meet more of your family."

"Today is special," I said. "My grandfather, on my mother's side, turns ninety-five. He plays eighteen holes of golf a day, three days a week."

"That is amazing," Dr. Manning said.

"I want to introduce you to two of my friends. This is Dice," I said.

"Hello," Dice said.

"Nice to meet you," Dr. Manning said.

"And this is Maks," I said.

"Hello," Maks said.

"Nice to meet you, too," Dr. Manning said.

"The three of us went fishing yesterday," I said. "We really wore the fish out. Dice, how many do you think we caught?"

"I don't know," Dice said. "It was a lot."

"Where did you go?" Dr. Manning asked.

"To the Gulf Stream," I said.

"That is a big trip," Dr. Manning said. "I have not fished offshore in years. Which boat did you charter?"

"Dad's," I said.

I gave Dr. Manning a summary account of our trip, leaving out the most traumatic details.

"Do you have life insurance?" Dr. Manning asked.

"No," I said.

"You need to get life insurance. It is easy. I can do the medical screening at no cost. The insurance company pays for it."

"You're probably right. How much does it cost?"

"You can get a million dollars in coverage for about fifty to sixty dollars a month."

"A million dollars!" I said.

"Yes."

"A million dollars!" I said. All of a sudden, I felt rich. I counted the money in my head and thought of all the ways my family could use it. This was it, I thought. This is the investment that might make my family rich. Then I realized that the investment required that I be dead. And then I realized that I did not yet have life insurance and I thought of how bad off Lynn and Tyler and Sophia would be if I died without life insurance.

"I wouldn't get too excited about it," Dr. Manning said, "but everyone with children should have life insurance."

"You're right. I'll get it soon," I said, "but chances are that I will not need it, especially if I got my Grandpapa's genes."

Our group of men stood around talking while friends and family mingled about the house. At some point, Pastor David showed up.

"Hello, Pastor David," I said. "It is good to see you here."

He nodded and joined our group. I thought, this is a motley crew—me, Dr. Manning, Pastor David, Silent Maks, and the Wild Weasel—but it was a good crew, and I was pleased to celebrate Grandpapa's birthday with my friends, both old and new. It was then I realized that I did not have many friends that lived nearby. I had been so busy working and fixing my house and raising kids that there just was not time to make many friends.

"Guys, do you want to see a real treasure?" I asked.

"Sure," Dice said.

"You know about the treasure?" Pastor David asked.

"This way," I said. "It's in here. Look over there."

Grandpapa sat on the couch in our living room, holding his small pet dog. Grandpapa went everywhere with that dog. They could not be separated. Grandpapa stayed seated and quiet while family and friends mingled about. He dozed in and out of sleep, not saying a word.

"That's him," I said. "That's my Grandpapa."

"He still plays golf?" Dr. Manning asked.

"Three days a week," I said.

"Look at his hands," Dr. Manning said.

Grandpapa's hands looked like knots on an ancient cypress stump. He sat there quiet, every now and then petting his dog.

"He is legally deaf and blind," I said, "but I know he can see and hear. He just can't hear anything with all this noise. He can hear so long as it is one person talking to him. When the crowd leaves the room, let's go talk to him."

A few minutes later, the crowd departed, taking their conversation to another room. It was just Grandpapa and us.

"Go ask him about the Democrats," I told Dice.

"Why?" Dice asked.

"He hates them."

"No. I wouldn't dare," Dice said.

"Then go ask him about the Republicans," I said.

"Why?" Dice asked.

"He hates them too."

"No. I don't like confrontation," Dice said.

"Fine. Go ask him about football. He's a huge fan of Clemson football."

"You do it," Dice said.

"Hey, Grandpapa," I said. "How is Clemson going to do this year?"

"Huh? Clemson. They'll do all right, I guess. But we gotta stop sending all these crooks to Warshington, taking our money to pay for all them agencies in DC. Dey's thousands of them, all in Warshington. Most of 'em ain't worth a flip. But some are. I know how a person can win the next presidency. Guaranteed! A hunnert percent! But ain't nobody care 'bout what an ole man gotta say. Dey all talk 'bout draining the swamp and we all know that ain't never gonna happen, what dey gotta do is spread the swamp! Ain't no reason to have all dem agencies in one place. Spread it about America just like the internet and you'll win America and we'll be better for it and it will be America that's gubberning itself. I knows good people in my town who would love a good paying federal job and they'd be good at it too. How would you like to work for the State Department or the FBI or some other overgrown agency from yer hometown? We could do it, too, if them crooks had to shake yer hand first and look you in the eyes before gettin a vote, like it use to be. That was before robots started calling me on the phone. I had a gubberment job once—in the wahr. I was in the Merchant Marine, but they never gave me nothing and I ain't never asked, but I should have! I was on a Liberty ship and der was thousands of us. They built one every day. We was sittin ducks durin the whole wahr. The only reason I didn't get blown up was because they was so many of us to choose from. And we couldn't fight back because we ain't had nothing for guns. That's why I joined the Merchant Marine in da fuhrst place. I told the recruiter that I couldn't shoot a man. This ain't had nothing to do with guns. I hunted all the time, so much that people thought I lived in the woods, but I never did shoot no deer, something about their eyes. I could never bring myself to do it, probably cause I saw that dead body near Perry's. My grandmother had a house and all of us kids used to play in and around it. It ain't there no more, been gone a long time, but the bigger kids were always teasing us and playing tricks and they knew they could trick me and I was easy to trick and probably only about sebben years old when they told me to go into the shed and get dem something, I don't remember what it was they wanted but that's no matter cause dey said they needed me to get it and so I did and when I went into that shed, there was a dead man laid across the table just a looking up with his dead eyes and he'd been dead awhile I think and I don't know why but he was in there and somebody put him there, maybe just waiting to bury him but it scared me. I was just a boy but I remember those dead eyes just like it happened this morning and it scared me so and maybe it was that or maybe it wasn't but I told that recruiter that I couldn't shoot anyone so they put me on a Liberty ship with no guns. I liked the ship and being out at sea and I loved to just drive that ship and stare out at sea and never really got scared but I should have been since we didn't have anything for weapons and we was so slow. We crossed the Atlantic and I got to see It'ly and went to Venice and did you know the streets are made of water there and you travel by boat and we had never seen anything like it and stayed all day and into the night and when it got too late we started back to our ship in a little dinghy but the seas picked up and capsized our little boat and my friend couldn't swim very well and I could swim all right and I remember grabbing his shirt when he started to go under but the waves knocked us apart and we all looked for him but never found him. He was a good man, but too young and really just a boy and I was too and that was toward the end of my service. All we had to do was get back to the States and we did. We sailed back to New Orleans and my service time had ended two weeks before we left the port of New Orleans and I told my captain he was taking me back to shore and he laughed but he ain't laughed fer long cause he knew I was serious and he did take me back and just slowed the boat enough fer me to jump off and I did with my seabag that had everything I owned. Then I caught a train and went to Clemson and told them I wanted to go to college and they said ok so I did and back then there warn't no girls at Clemson and that was too bad for us but I met yer grandmother there. She was nearby and I knew I would do anything for that woman and I did. I got a job and I worked at it fer forty-four years and I only did that fer my wife and fer my daughters and dey is the best daughters a man could have and I have the best grandchildren a man could have and I know it and I tell everyone 'bout my grandchildren and I tell them the truth and dey don't believe me but that's ok. I got good friends and dey take me to play golf, every Monday and Wednesday and dey drive the cart up to the ball for me since I can't see it and I wish I could drive myself to the course and I do sometimes eben though I don't have no license on account of being blind but I can feel my way through town cause I'm as ole as that town and knows it and dey all know me. I's hoping to get me a self-driving car someday. That way I can just tell the car whar to go instead of telling my friends but I don't think Warshington will let us have self-driving cars anytime soon on account of dem all being crooks and in the pockets of whoever has da most money and it ain't always been this way. Der was a time when the crooks had to shake yer hand before getting a vote and I knows how to fix it too! Dey need to spread that swamp all over America so it is actually run by America and if you want to be president den all you has to do is say you gonna bring all those good gubberment jobs to America! And you would win! But ain't nobody care 'bout what an ole man has to say. I only been around longer than everbody else and seen the Great Depression and every recession and wahr since then and I don't want none of you runnin for president anyway cause that's so hard on yer family and the country will just try to tear you apart and I don't wish that on no one and I'm getting tired now and wish you warn't have got me started 'bout politics and would rather talk 'bout football. . . . Do you think Clemson is going to play Alabama this year? . . . Dey probably will. . . . We'll see . . ."

Then he closed his eyes and drifted back off to sleep.

I whispered to the others, "He had three heart attacks and cancer twice. That was thirty years ago. I bet he will still be golfing at one hundred. This side of my family lives forever. I hope I have his genes."

## CHAPTER 30

# A Letter to Silent Maks
## and the Wild Weasel

*M*aks & Dice - *I'm writing you to let you know what happened over the past few days.*

*About three days ago, we came home after a week of visiting with Lynn's parents and our neighbor Otis brought us our mail. But he needed help bringing some of the other packages. One was in a wheelbarrow and he and I agreed that it was the heaviest box of diapers we'd ever seen. We got it through the door and I told Lynn to come get her stuff. It struck me as a little bit odd that the diapers went "clank" when I set the box down. Had I investigated further and bothered to look at the side of the box, I would have immediately realized that I was now the proud owner of someone else's Lowcountry Classic Model C468 Fish Cooker with a Cast-Iron Dutch Oven, not to mention the Heavy Duty Electric Fillet Knife (Couteau a filets electrique) by HamsKnives.*

*Instead of looking at the box, Otis and I tore into it, discovering the fish cooker and electric knife.*

*"You sure you didn't order it?" I asked Otis.*

*He swore it was not his and that he got it off my porch and I told him that I didn't order it but I would keep it anyway and thought we should close the door before the owner came looking for it. I quickly called the kids to come see my birthday present. Tyler reminded me that it was not my birthday or even close to my birthday but I told him those details did not matter and to look at this really cool knife we now have. I did not let Sophia hold the knife.*

*Twenty-two seconds later, the kids moved on. But I was still confused by the whole event.*

*Mystery solved! I called my dad to thank him for the excellent gift. He, of course, being modest and all, pretended that he did not give me any such gift. I accused him of being a liar and old and losing his mind from working too much, until I realized that he really wasn't that modest and was probably telling the truth.*

*"Well, maybe I drank way too much the other night and bought it off Lynn's online account," I told him. That made perfect sense to both of us. I felt a renewed sense of peace and satisfaction, knowing that I had actually purchased these items and had not stolen them from anyone.*

*Dad said something about asking your pals to see if they bought it but I quickly reminded him that I don't have any pals or really know anyone in the area and he was the only person on the planet that would know I needed an electric fillet knife and a fish cooker.*

*In the end, Dad said he would take credit for the gift, and this pleased us both, although his willingness to take credit for it cast doubt on my I-drank-too-much theory.*

*The next day: I put the ordeal to the side to work and help my wife keep our children fed and alive. I treated Tyler's knee. A few days prior he had sliced it to the bone, kneecap hanging out, skin flapping, blood everywhere, but he is recovering nicely.*

*The next day: Same.*

*About thirty minutes ago: I took a break from surviving to put this thing together so I could get ready to cook some fish, even though it might not happen for a while, but I thought I should be ready for it when it does. In an uncharacteristic display of thoroughness, I looked for an instruction manual. Son-of-a-bleep. I found a note that said, "Thank you for the fishing trip—Maks & Dice."*

*My mind raced quickly to the day after our trip when we were sawing at the fish with spoons and a dull knife in the hot sun and then trying to cook them with a pair of forks and a cheap frying pan. Both of you were there. Finally, mystery solved. Thank you.*

*Unnecessary, but the coolest gift ever. Let's use it soon. - Mel*

CHAPTER 31

# *The Old Man Knows*

"The old man knows!" Mori said, sitting down with Judd at the dark bar.

"The old man knows what?" Judd asked.

Mori leaned over.

"The old man knows where the gold is. I'm sure of it. Look at these," Mori said, "I found them at a pawn shop."

Mori showed Judd three golden coins, all marked with a spear piercing a heart.

"They look just like the one on Charcoal's necklace," Judd said.

"That's right," Mori said, putting the coins back in his pocket and giving Judd a wink.

"Never doubt me," Mori said. "Running across these coins required a bit of luck, but I have staked out that crazy old man's booth on River Street for weeks. He sells shark teeth, but I think it's a cover. He has a girlfriend, a witch of sorts that reads palms and talks to the dead. A total fraud, I'm sure, but that does not concern us. That old man knows where the gold is. I'm certain of it. Folks around here told me he has been diving in the river for decades, gathering bones and shark teeth and selling them. He lives on an island on the marsh, living off the water and land. Just as crazy as a loon from what I can tell, but he knows where the gold is."

"Where is it?"

"I don't know. That's the only piece I don't know yet, but I will. We are going to follow him out to his island one night, at the right time, but not yet. We need to shake this Charcoal fellow first."

"How?"

"You leave that to me. Just stay quiet and let me do the talking when he gets here."

"Ok."

"There's more," Mori said, taking a sip of his drink. "That crazy old man has been running with an even crazier old man. A preacher or something. Anyway, he gives the preacher a gold coin every week. That is who has been pawning the coins."

"The preacher?"

"His wife," Mori said. "She is the only normal one in the bunch. They are a strange crew, but they will lead us to that gold. You just watch."

Across the dark bar, a door opened.

"Here comes Charcoal. You stay quiet," Mori said.

"Hello, gentlemen," Charcoal said, taking his seat.

"Hello," Mori said.

"Tonight is the night. We have slack currents," Charcoal said. "The gear is ready. What did you learn about the crazy old man?"

"Just that," Mori said. "He's crazy. His name is Jesse Turner and he lives on an island in the marsh. He has lived there for almost forty years. No job or nothing. He lives off shrimp and fish and has no use for money. I don't think he would know what to do with a gold coin if he had one."

"That is about what I figured," Charcoal said. "If anyone had found that gold, the whole world would have heard about it already. I think it is gone, probably buried out here on some island. But just to be thorough, I'll dive tonight and see if I can find anything the submersible missed. I doubt I will."

Charcoal took a sip of his drink.

"I'm sorry, guys," Charcoal said. "I appreciate all your help, but if we don't find any gold tonight, then I am leaving first thing tomorrow morning. My wife will not let me stay any longer, especially if the gold is lost."

"No hard feelings," Mori said. "It has been a good ride and we understood the chances getting into it. I'll just go back to fishing. I have not lost anything but time."

"Well, let's meet back here at dusk," Charcoal said. "Maybe we'll find something interesting."

At dusk, the three men met at the bar.

"Ready?" Charcoal asked.

"Let's do it," Mori said.

The three men boarded Charcoal's yacht and then unloaded the small dark boat. They eased through the night to the deep hole. At dead low tide, Charcoal, put on top-of-the-line diving equipment, including lights and night-vision cameras. He dove down to the ship and he stayed down for an hour before surfacing.

"Find anything?" Mori asked after Charcoal surfaced.

"Nothing," Charcoal said. "The ship is there. I could feel it, but there's no gold. The submersible was right."

"We tried," Mori said.

"We tried," Charcoal said. "That is the blackest, darkest water I have ever been in and I could barely fight the current when the tide changed. Part of me is glad we did not find any gold. I'm not sure how we could get it up. That hole is not for humans."

Charcoal put his equipment to the side.

"Let's ride back," Charcoal said. "There is no use wasting any more time out here."

They eased back to Savannah. The next morning, Charcoal's yacht was gone.

CHAPTER 32

# *A Slump*

It is hard to be a little league baseball coach, especially when your team is terrible. We were on track to set a record as the worst baseball team ever. No one on our team could hit the ball, which was understandable when you consider the fact that the pitching machine was hurling the ball at over forty miles per hour and the oldest kid on the team was six.

"I should have put more thought into picking the team," Coach Ryan, the head coach, said.

"Yeah," I said, looking at the scoreboard. The game had been called at 20 to 0.

"I thought that it was all about having fun and teaching the kids how to play," Coach Ryan said.

"Nope," I said.

"I can tell that the kids want to win. I really wish we had a chance to win just one game," he said.

"Yeah, winning is fun. This season will be a life lesson for these kids. They will learn how to lose."

"We need to do something," he said. "Maybe you could ask your preacher friend to pray for us?"

Pastor David had made it a habit of following me around the neighborhood and to baseball games and to different events. I'm not sure why he did so but I suspect it was because I never turned him away. That was ok with me. He was not my first weird friend.

Weird people had always been attracted to me, perhaps because of my own weirdness, but I do not think that was why. I think it had more to do with me treating them as a human being, which was not the custom in either middle school or high school. My abnormal approach to weird people found its roots in a birthday party in the sixth grade. Like every class in America, there was one kid in our class that was exceptionally weird. His name was Gilbert Lyle. For the most part, I ignored Gilbert. There was no mal intent in it. Gilbert and I simply did not share the same interests. I liked to play football and he liked to, well, I do not know what Gilbert liked to do because he was, uh, weird. Other kids noticed Gilbert's weirdness and took it upon themselves to tease him with no regard to whether he was present or not. I did not tease Gilbert, nor did I defend him. I simply went about sixth grade in a bliss, oblivious to pretty much everything. At some point during the year, I got an invitation to Gilbert's birthday party. So did the entire class. As usual, I thought nothing of it. My mother can take credit for what happened next.

I remember sitting with her at our kitchen table, staring at the invitation. I was torn.

"Well, it's your choice," Mom said. "You can either go to Gilbert's birthday party or go hunting with your dad."

More than anything, I wanted to go hunting. Rut had just begun, causing all the male deer to go mad for all the female deer. Free from all inhibitions and sense of self-preservation, the male deer crashed through the woods in hopes of stumbling across a female deer they had not yet met that rut. Naturally, this caused male humans to rush to the woods in hopes of killing one of the male deer, a phenomenon that has existed since the beginning of time.

"Is Gilbert one of your good friends?" Mom asked.

"No."

"Did he invite many people?"

"The whole class, but I don't think many people will go."

"Why not?"

"Gilbert gets picked on a lot."

"I see. Well, it looks like he lives quite a ways from here."

"I don't know."

"I'll take you there if you choose to go."

"Ok. I'll go. I guess I can go hunting next weekend."

Mom took me to Gilbert's house. He lived in a small house on a dirt road way out in the woods. No other kids lived nearby. Gilbert's mom had baked a cake and bought balloons and prepared to host a couple dozen kids. Gilbert sat at the empty table smiling as if the whole class were about to show up in any minute. To my recollection, Gilbert always wore that smile, even when mean kids teased him.

After about thirty minutes, it was clear that no one else was coming. It was just Gilbert and me. He showed me around his house and yard and we played basketball, despite Gilbert being terrible at basketball, and we played baseball, despite Gilbert being terrible at baseball. All in all, we had a great time. Had Gilbert lived two doors down, I think we would have become friends.

On the way home from Gilbert's house, my mother said that she had never been prouder of me and my choice to go to Gilbert's and of how nice I was to Gilbert and how much it meant to Gilbert to be treated like a normal kid and my mother even cried on the ride home and I never knew why because I was in the sixth grade and clueless.

I also remember coming home to find Dad glowing with pride. He had shot a record ten-point buck and everyone—all ten men who went hunting—had bagged trophy bucks and he told me how he had never seen anything like that rut and that the deer he shot was so crazy and mad that it charged at him while he was walking through the woods and that he shot the buck to save himself and he went on and on about the great hunt and how he could not wait to take me next weekend. Well, we did go hunting the next weekend and saw nothing and heard nothing because rut had passed, having been compressed it seemed into a single day—the day I played with Gilbert. It was the kind of weekend a young boy does not forget.

Something about Pastor David on the baseball field made me think of Gilbert Lyle and I wondered if Gilbert still wore his big smile. I hoped so.

Despite his general aloofness, Pastor David found ways to help, shagging balls and carrying equipment and doing other various chores. More than anything, he just liked to watch the game. He seemed to want the kids to win, or at least score, more than anyone at the field, including the kids. The man liked baseball.

"I am going to do some research," Coach Ryan said. "These kids must learn how to hit the ball. At the next practice, we will focus solely on hitting the ball."

"Sounds good," I said.

I admired Coach Ryan's dedication. He had enough to do without having to coach a dozen hopeless six-year-olds. He was a senior enlisted man in the Army, in charge of hundreds of people and things and projects. Those were headaches enough. He had done very well in the Army, probably due to his extreme attention to detail and relentless dedication to mission accomplishment. These traits also served him well as a coach, but the lack of success frustrated him and he could not let it go.

Coach Ryan showed up to the next practice with four different manuals, each providing specific instructions on how to hit a baseball.

"Kids, today we are going to learn how to hit a baseball," Coach Ryan said. "These manuals are written by Hall of Fame baseball players. The men who wrote these manuals spent their lifetimes hitting baseballs and each of them has condensed his knowledge into an easy-to-follow manual."

Pastor David and I leaned against the fence, listening to Coach Ryan belt out the plan of the day.

"We will break out into four stations," Coach Ryan said. "At each station, you will work on your stance and swing. We will do nothing but work on hitting a baseball. That is our mission—to hit a baseball. Does everyone understand that?"

One kid raised his hand.

"Yes, Wesley. What is your question?" Coach Ryan asked.

"Coach Ryan, did you know that this morning I found a toad in my driveway? One of its legs was missing, but it could still hop so fast that I couldn't catch it and then my brother came outside and we . . ."

"Ok, Wesley. Thank you for that, but let's focus on learning how to hit a baseball, all right? Coach Mel and I will both man a station. I need two parent volunteers, each to man the other stations. I will leave a manual at each station. It has pictures and is easy to follow. Please use the manual to help your small group learn how to hit."

We dispersed to our four stations and spent the day trying to teach the kids how to hit like major leaguers.

"Align your first set of knuckles like this," I said. "No, your other first set of knuckles."

"Bend your knees," I said.

"Get your elbow up," I said.

Wesley raised his hand.

"Yes, Wesley?" I said.

"Coach Ryan told us to keep our elbow down," Wesley said.

"Well, this manual says to keep your elbow up," I said.

All the manuals had good advice, but they were inconsistent. Some said to hit the top of the ball, some said to hit the bottom of the ball. Some said to keep the bat up, some said to keep the bat down.

"I don't think this is working," I told Coach Ryan as we watched the kids struggle with all the details and inconsistencies.

"It's hopeless," he said. "I don't know what to do. We just have to keep trying. We can't stand back and watch these kids get slaughtered every game."

"I know," I said. "Maybe a few of them will come around."

The next day, I worked with Tyler on his hitting. I had played baseball all the way through high school and had continued to play softball for years later. I knew how to hit a ball, but I did not know how to teach someone else how to hit a ball.

"Tyler, do you want to learn how to hit a baseball?" I asked.

"Yes, Dad," he said.

"Let's go practice."

"Ok," he said.

"We'll call it a special practice," I said. "Just you and me, father and son, working on hitting a baseball."

"Ok, Dad."

In our yard, I threw pitch after pitch and Tyler missed pitch after pitch. I knew that our time together was limited, a six-year-old only having so long of an attention span. As was his custom, Pastor David showed up, which proved quite helpful. He chased down all the balls Tyler missed. Tyler's stance and swing seemed awkward.

"Dad, I'm tired of doing this. I want to do something else."

"Just a few more minutes," I pleaded.

"Ok," he said.

I threw a few more pitches and he missed them all. Tyler dropped the bat and sulked off.

"Tyler!" I said. "Just a few more minutes."

"No! Dad. I don't want to."

"I can help," I said. "All you need to do is listen to me."

"No! I don't want to."

I knew then I had made a fatal mistake. There was a reason I was assistant coach and not head coach. There was a reason I deferred to Coach Ryan and to the manuals and to anyone else who might try to help my son. I was his father. I had learned long ago that the last person a son wanted advice from was his father.

"Ok," I said. "We don't have to practice anymore. And you don't have to listen to me. But if you change your mind, just let me know. All you have to do is ask."

I picked up the bat.

"Pastor David!" I said. "Can you pitch?"

He nodded, picked up a few of the plastic balls, and walked toward me. He threw the first one.

I crushed it. It flew as far as a plastic ball could fly. He threw another. And I crushed it. Another. And I crushed it, splitting the ball in two. In between pitches, I noticed Tyler moving closer and closer. I put the bat down after splitting the ball in two.

"Dad?" Tyler asked. "How did you do that?"

"It's a secret," I said. "Don't worry about it. Go do something else. Pastor David and I will just stay here and crush some baseballs."

"Dad?" Tyler asked. "Can you tell me the secret, please?"

"Of course," I said, "all you had to do was ask your old man."

I kneeled down on one knee, holding a baseball. Pastor David walked over to us. It was one of the rare moments in my life where I had my son's undivided attention and I did not want to waste it.

"Everyone has a different swing," I said. "That is not important. It is hard to hit a baseball. And even those who know how to hit a baseball can get into a slump."

"What's a slump?" Tyler asked.

"It is when someone who knows how to hit a baseball forgets how to hit a baseball. No matter how much they practice and no matter how much advice they get, they cannot hit a baseball."

"Why?" Tyler asked.

"Well, it is hard to explain. See, no one can hit the ball for you. It is just one of those things in life that you have to do yourself. And you have to know the secret."

"Tell me the secret, Dad! Tell me!"

"Son," I said. "It's simple. All you have to do is believe that you can hit it. If you believe that you can hit it, then you will see the ball. And if you see the ball, you can hit it. I promise. That's it. Want to try?"

"Yes," he said.

I threw the first pitch. He missed. I threw another. And he missed. But he stayed in there.

I heard him whisper to himself, "I believe." Pastor David heard it too.

I threw another pitch and he crushed it.

"Wow, kid!" I said. "Look at that!"

I threw another pitch. And he crushed it. He was smiling now. I watched him crush pitch after pitch after pitch. I knew that he could do it, but I had no idea that the transformation would be so sudden. I was amazed.

During the next game, Tyler went three for three, but the rest of the team could not get a hit. At the following game, the same thing happened.

"What got into Tyler?" Coach Ryan asked.

"I'm not exactly sure," I said. "We were practicing at home and, all of a sudden, he started hitting the ball. I think he can just see it now."

Soon, Tyler was nine for nine. I tried to tell him that he had done something that even the greatest players could not do, but this was lost on him. He now just assumed that he was supposed to get a hit every time. Then the inevitable happened; during the next game—he struck out.

As the first base coach, I had a front-row seat to his strikeout. When it happened, I almost laughed, because I knew that his streak would end. In fact, I felt somewhat relieved that it did end. Nine for nine was almost too much. I did not laugh, however, because my little boy came running down the first-base line crying, emotional, and unable to understand what had just happened.

I got down on one knee and held him.

"Kid," I said, smiling as tears ran down his dirty face. "I know you're upset, but you just did something amazing. You went nine for ten. Someday you'll realize how special that is. No one does that. But everyone strikes out. You will get another chance. Go back to the dugout and get ready for your next at-bat."

Still confused, he wiped the tears off his face and went back to his team. Others, parents and kids alike, had noticed Tyler's hitting streak. They wanted to know how he had all of a sudden turned into a hitting machine. I couldn't explain it. He was hot and could see the ball. It was that simple to me.

"We play the Braves on Friday night," Coach Ryan said. "Except for Tyler, our team is still terrible."

"I know," I said.

"I wish we could have just won one game. None of them were even close."

"I know."

"The Braves are undefeated."

"I know."

"It is going to be a massacre."

"I know."

Friday night brought in crisp, cool air. Pastor David, Tyler, and I went to the baseball field one last time for the season. The field smelled of fresh cut grass. It was a perfect night for baseball.

"Tyler," I said, "no matter what happens today, I want you to know that I am proud of you. You have done very well this season."

"Thanks, Dad."

"I'm not just proud because you did well, I'm proud because you did not give up. That means more than how many hits you got."

"Thanks, Dad."

"I just wish we could have won a game," I said.

"We still have one left," he said. "I wish the other kids could hit the ball too. It is no fun to lose."

"I agree, kid," I said.

The game began exactly as we all expected. As the leadoff batter, Tyler crushed one to the outfield but stood alone on second base as our next three batters struck out. Meanwhile, the Braves scored at will.

In the dugout, I heard one of the players ask Tyler, "How do you know how to hit the ball so well?"

"It's a secret," Tyler said.

"Really? Tell me," the other player said.

"Sure," Tyler said.

Tyler leaned over and whispered, "You have to believe you can hit it. Just tell yourself that 'you believe' and you'll hit it."

The other kid's eyes lit up as if Tyler had actually given him something special, like a jewel or a piece of gold or something valuable only known to them.

I laughed to myself. Kids. It was cute and it got cuter. As the other kid got up to bat, I watched him quietly repeat to himself, "I believe."

Dumbfounded, the crowd watched the ball fly over the shortstop's head and into the outfield, rolling all the way to the fence. Then the crowd erupted into a roar.

"Run!" Coach Ryan yelled. "Run!"

Stunned, the kid stood at home plate as the other team ran after the ball he had just crushed.

"Run!" Coach Ryan yelled.

The kid raced to first base. I sent him to second, where he stopped.

The crowd went absolutely nuts. Parents started throwing things into the air in celebration. Someone other than Tyler had hit the ball.

Another player waiting to bat had seen Tyler and the other kid talking right before the kid crushed the ball.

"What did you tell him?" the other player asked.

"A secret," Tyler said.

"Tell me," the other player asked.

Tyler whispered the secret to the other player and I watched the other player's eyes light up just like the player before him. Like the first kid, the player quietly repeated to himself, "I believe. I believe. I believe."

He launched the next pitch to right field.

"Run!" Coach Ryan yelled. "Run!"

The kid on second base rounded third and headed for home. You could feel the excitement when he stepped on home plate. Parents shouted and jumped up and down and carried on like a bunch of children. I can only imagine what the other team thought. It was only one run.

Tyler's secret spread like wildfire. I stood amazed as the kids whispered the secret to each other, repeating the simple phrase, "I believe." I found it to be a little silly but I dared not interfere. The kids believed in a way that only a child's mind can believe. And it worked. Kid after kid smacked pitch after pitch, scoring run after run. We were in the game.

It was the bottom of the last inning. There were two outs. The score was tied, with the winning run on third. It was Tyler's turn to bat. As Tyler walked up to the plate, I started walking toward him. I wanted to tell him to enjoy the moment and to have fun and to be proud of what he and his team had done, no matter what happened.

I took a few steps toward him and stopped.

Tyler walked straight to the plate and got in his stance, his eyes laser focused on the pitching machine.

Resisting all the urges that come with being a dad and wanting to help my child, I went back to first base. He was on his own.

The first pitch came in low. Tyler swung and missed.

Dammit, I thought. This is one hell of a time for the machine to be off.

The umpire adjusted the machine and fired off the next pitch.

It came in high. Tyler swung and missed.

The players in both dugouts rose to their feet and clung to the fence. The parents rose to their feet. Pastor David rose to his feet. Random bystanders rose to their feet. Everyone rose to their feet. We knew this was it. The last pitch. All the kids swung at every pitch. They did not know any better because they were kids, six-year-olds.

For a moment, we had forgotten about how horrible we were supposed to be. For a moment, we had forgotten that we had scored the first run of the season just a few innings ago. For a moment, we had forgotten that Tyler was just a six-year-old kid with no idea how much pressure rested on his shoulders during that final pitch.

I looked at Tyler. He remained focused on the machine. The rest of the world disappeared around him. He did not hear the roar or the noise behind him. He could not feel the ground shake beneath him. He kept his eyes on the machine and on the ball and on nothing else.

The umpire fired off the last pitch. I never saw the ball. I was watching Tyler. There appeared to be no doubt in the kid's mind. He knew he would hit the ball. He possessed a supernatural confidence in the moment. I did not have such faith. I feared he would miss and I wondered how he would respond to the loss. It was too much for a six-year-old, I thought. It was too much for me, so I closed my eyes.

I have heard few sweeter sounds in life than the crack of that bat. And the roar that followed was unforgettable. But to my dying day, I will remember, more than anything, the sight of Tyler running toward me, smiling with his eyes aglow in the night lights. It was the kind of joy every parent and every child deserves to know.

We won, 19 to 18. Our team rejoiced, but none more than Pastor David. The game had taken an exceptional toll on him. As our team huddled together to celebrate the win, I watched Pastor David walk to the corner of the outfield and kneel. I could tell he was crying. It must have been out of joy. The man loved baseball.

## CHAPTER 33

# Life Insurance

The air turned cold, a sign that one of Savannah's four-day winters was approaching.

I finally got around to applying for life insurance for my family. I found I could get one million dollars in life insurance for about fifty dollars a month. Sure, it was expensive, but for one million dollars of peace of mind, I thought it was worth it.

I drove toward Dr. Manning's office to finish the final screening. After that, my family would be set. I no longer feared leaving them behind, burdened with all of my bad decisions. And I could work at a lousy job for the rest of my life like almost everyone else. In fact, I now felt lucky to have that lousy job. We were getting by and if I thought about it more, we were living the high life. I had a house and a van and I had a job and my family was happy. I had made two good friends in Dr. Manning and Pastor David.

Pastor David had come full circle, more so really. His congregation said it was a miracle. They wondered how he had suddenly transformed from an erratic, aloof, and absent-minded wanderer into a confident, caring, and understanding leader of the church. For me, he had become an even better friend.

Dr. Manning had gone out of his way to help, too, walking me through the various injuries and illnesses that had plagued my family. Now, under the umbrella of a life insurance screening, he had been conducting additional tests it seemed—x-rays, blood tests, and a CT scan. There was no doubt he was giving me an extra physical that I could not otherwise afford.

Sipping my morning coffee, I drove along the long highway looking across the wide marsh. Yes, I thought, we had made it. We were making it work. This was living.

I walked into Dr. Manning's office and greeted the receptionist.

"Hello, Mr. Scott," she said.

"Good morning," I said.

"I will let Dr. Manning know you are here. He wants you to do one more CT scan first. Please come with me."

"Another test?" I asked. "He sure is thorough."

"Yes, he is a good doctor. Please come with me."

Dr. Manning made sure I got special treatment. I did not sit in a waiting room. His polite staff escorted me directly to the imaging room, where the technician was waiting for me.

"This will only take a minute, Mr. Scott," the technician said. "Where is your pain?"

"Pain?" I said. "I don't have any pain."

She seemed confused.

"Unless you are talking about my job and my kids and my house," I joked. "They are about forty miles away."

She smiled, but did not laugh.

"This is just for a life insurance screening," I said.

"I see. It will only take a minute and you will not feel a thing."

After completing the scan, she escorted me to a private evaluation room.

I did not have time to sit down before Dr. Manning walked in.

"Good morning, doc," I said.

"Good morning, Mel."

"Thank you for the five-star treatment."

"You are welcome. Mel, please sit down. How are you feeling this morning?"

I detected an unusually somber tone in his voice.

"What's going on, doc? I am starting to feel like I am here on a sick visit, not a screening."

"Mel, I am going to give you the news straight and unfiltered. That is my job as your doctor. But I am also your friend, which makes this the most difficult conversation I have ever had to have."

"Is there something, some kind of pre-existing condition, that prevents me from getting life insurance?"

"Yes."

"I see. What is it, doc?"

"You have cancer."

I sat stunned.

"It is all over. I saw it on the first set of scans and did not want to believe it. But all the tests have confirmed that you have cancer."

"How bad is it?"

"It is all over your body, Mel. It is on your lungs, on your kidneys, on your liver, on your brain. Mel, it is everywhere."

"What does this mean? How do we treat it?"

"Mel, it is not treatable."

"How long do I have?"

"Mel, it is a medical miracle that you are still walking and talking and breathing right now. I have already looked into hospice care for you and can help you with that if you choose."

"I don't have the money."

"I can help."

"This can't happen yet. Not this soon," I said. "I can't leave my wife and children with all this debt."

"I'm so sorry, Mel. Please, let me take you home. I cleared my schedule. I can drive you home."

"Thank you, but I need to drive myself. I don't want Lynn or the kids to see you driving me home. They will know something is wrong. I need to make some money quick. Do you think I will make it thirty days?"

"Mel, I know this is tough and there is nothing I can say to make it easier. Dying is different for everyone. I have been beside the beds of thousands of patients who were passing away and I have been a witness to many of their last words. I cannot tell you what to do with the time you have left but I can tell you without hesitation that no one has ever said, 'I wish I had worked more in life.' The last wish of the dying is almost universal. Almost everyone says, 'I wish I would have spent more time with my family and my loved ones.' What you do in your final days is your choice. Just let me know how I can help."

CHAPTER 34

*The Collapse*

The fog around me thickened as I drove home. All the buildings and cars and people and things disappeared. I thought of nothing else but Dr. Manning's words. "It's all over." I did not want to believe it. But I knew it was true. I could feel it now. I could feel the dull pains inside my body. I felt each pain with every bump in the road. How had I missed this before? If only I had more time. I needed more time. But I knew it was all over. I would leave my family with nothing but debt. No health insurance. No savings. No anything. It was all over. I could not accept this. I could not let it end without a fight. I needed to do something.

Traffic came to a halt. Somehow, so did my car. I no longer made decisions for my hands and feet. Their movements were now involuntary and separate from my mind. I looked at my watch as I sat in traffic. Seconds ticked away. I sat in traffic as more seconds ticked away. I knew I only had so many seconds left and each one counted. I could no longer bear to see them tick away.

I threw my watch out the window. That helped, I thought. Counting time no longer mattered. I needed to focus on one thing. I now had one singular mission in life. It was clear, more so than ever before. I needed money. I needed to leave my family with money.

Maybe I had a few days left before the worst pain set in. Maybe not. How could I make money now? I needed a moonshot. Just the hope and prospect of money would help. The magic penny, I thought. That is it. The magic penny. I knew it was possible. I needed to find something that would double and double again and double again. Something that would last beyond my time. And I needed to start with more than a penny. I needed money.

I knew I could not go home yet. Lynn would know something was wrong and I could not waste precious time at home. I needed to find money. I drove in circles it seemed until I ended up in the parking lot of Pastor David's church. What am I doing here? It was as if something else now controlled my body. My mind had moved on. It focused on one thing—money.

I sat exhausted in my car, but with my mind racing through all the ways I might make money. Fatigue set in and I could no longer stay awake. The fog still thick, I drifted off to sleep.

Maybe it was the weariness or the cancer or something else, but my dreams no longer took the shape of ordinary dreams. I could feel pain in my dreams, physical pain. I could taste and smell in my dreams. And the people were real, more so than in real life. They could walk in and out of my dreams like one could walk in and out of a room. It was all so vivid and well defined but I knew I was dreaming or at least semiconscious or in some state of in between. I knew I was dreaming but could not wake my body. I could reason and think and read in my dreams, and I did all those things in search of one thing—money. But I knew I was dreaming because in my dreams there was no fog. All was clear. In my dreams, there was no time and no rush. Seconds and minutes and hours and years no longer mattered. Time and space disappeared. There was no need for clocks or cars.

I moved about in my dreams with ease, from person to person and from place to place. In my dreams, I saw my family and friends, living and unaware that it was all over. I also saw old friends and familiar faces with names I had long forgotten. In my dreams, I saw my dad's father and his father and family members from long ago. The ones who had passed away knew I was dying. My dad's grandfather, who had died years before I was born, walked over to me.

"You need to tell Lynn," he said. "She needs to know."

"You're right," I said.

"She is strong," he said.

"I know," I said, "but I need to make some money first. She likes plans and certainty. I need a plan before I leave her. I want to leave her with hope."

"It is too late for a plan," he said. "That is for you, not her. Go see your family."

My dad's grandfather walked away and disappeared into my dreams. The conversation was real. There was no mistaking that, but it was also a dream. I went about my dreams searching for the answer, seeking advice from those who had died long ago. None shared my sense of urgency or concern.

I continued my search for some way to make money. It was my singular focus. I knew there was a way and I would not give up. Then I heard her voice behind me. I had heard it before and it stopped me in my tracks.

"You still have time," she said, "not much, but you still have time."

I turned around and saw the little girl, about six years old it seemed. She had a kind face and a warm smile. She was happy and in no hurry.

"There you are," I said.

"Welcome," she said, "I have been looking forward to meeting you."

"I know this is only a dream," I said.

"Of course it is only a dream, silly," she said, "but you need to wake up soon."

"I know, but it is so much easier to think in my dreams. I need to find a way to make money."

"Is that what you want?" she asked.

"Yes, more than anything."

"Well, go see Danny, silly."

"You're right. Thank you."

"And take Pastor David with you."

"Why?"

"You'll see. Tell him what has happened."

"Ok."

I heard a loud knocking next to my head.

Knock. Knock. Knock.

"Mel, are you ok? Mel!" It was Pastor David's voice.

I woke up in the seat of my car, still at the church, still surrounded by fog. It felt like I had been asleep for days.

"Hello, Pastor David," I said, opening the door.

"What happened? What are you doing here?" he asked.

"I'll tell you soon. How long have I been here?"

"I don't know. Not long. The parking lot was empty thir-ty minutes ago."

"I need your help," I said.

"With what?"

"I'm not sure yet," I said, "I need to go to Danny's right now. Will you ride with me?"

"Yes."

"Can you please call Lynn and tell her I'll be home late tonight?"

"Yes, but why don't you call her?"

"I can't. She will know something is wrong."

"Ok. What if she asks me what is going on?"

"Tell her what you know, that we are driving to Savannah to see Danny."

"Ok."

Pastor David made the call and returned to the parking lot.

"What did she say?" I asked.

"Not much. She said that was good and that Danny could probably use our help."

"Odd," I said. "Let's go. Can you drive?"

"Yes."

As Pastor David drove to Danny's, I told him that I was dying of cancer and that it was all over my body and that I needed to find money because I could not leave Lynn and my children with so much debt and that I spoke to a little girl in my dreams and I had heard her voice before when I almost crashed on the highway and other times too and that she told me to tell him what I knew and to go see Danny and there were others from the past in my dreams and I spoke to them too and it was all clear in my dreams but now everything was a fog again and it was hard to think and I felt the cancer now that I knew about it.

"Maybe Danny can help," I told Pastor David. "He has millions and it hurts me to ask him for anything, but I'm desperate and I'm not asking for me, I'm asking for Lynn and Tyler and Sophia. I can put my pride to the side this one time. He could spare a million dollars without ever knowing it. I'm hoping he will put it in a trust for my family, maybe to get the kids through high school. Then he can take it all back. It might even be worth more by then."

Pastor David nodded.

Still exhausted, I felt myself slipping back into a dream.

"We're here," Pastor David said.

I rubbed my eyes to make sure I could see. The gates were open. Large moving trucks lined Danny's driveway.

"This is it," I said. "Just drive down the long driveway. His house is at the end."

Danny stood on his front porch, talking to some guys carrying furniture.

"Mel!" Danny said.

"Hey, Danny," I said.

"Can you believe this?" he said, chuckling to himself.

"Believe what? What happened?" I asked.

"What do you mean, 'what happened'? Where have you been, living in a cave? Dude, the market crashed today. The single biggest loss in history and it is going to be worse tomorrow when they allow trading again. I saw it coming weeks ago. I had everything in one company and they went under. Then all my other income dried up. Now, I can't pay the taxes on this house," he said, still smiling.

"I don't know what to say, Danny," I said.

"Don't worry about me," Danny said. "I know what it is like to have nothing. I prefer it that way most of the time. That way I don't have to be responsible for anything."

"This is terrible," I said.

"Cheer up, man. You look worse than I do. The sun will rise again tomorrow. Look at her now," he said, pointing at the setting sun across the marsh. All the land and water lit up with brilliant colors of red and orange and yellow against a soft blue, violet sky.

"There is nothing like it, man," he said. "And it is free for all of us."

The three of us stood in Danny's yard watching the giant ball of fire disappear across the marsh.

"Mel," Pastor David said. "We need to go."

"Where?" I asked.

"River Street. Before all the vendors leave. We need to hurry."

"Ok," I said. "Good luck, Danny."

"That is what I'm counting on. See you, brother."

CHAPTER 35

# *Hail Mary*

Pastor David ran to the car and I followed. "You need to meet someone," he said. "I think I know why that little girl wanted me to go with you."

We rushed to River Street, parked the car, and ran down the old cobblestone road.

"There she is!" Pastor David said.

We slowed our run and walked to her booth.

"Hi, Ruby," Pastor David said. "Hello, Jesse."

"Hello, Pastor," Ruby said. "I thought you might stop by. You know, a giant red moon rises tonight. It will be one to remember."

"Hello, Jesse," I said.

"Hi, Mel. It is good to see you again. What brings you here?" Jesse asked.

"You know each other?" Pastor David asked.

"We've met," Jesse said. "I grew up with Mel's father."

"Ruby," Pastor David said. "I brought Mel here to talk to you. I think you can help him."

"Is that so?" she said, taking a seat and looking at me. "Mr. Scott, right?"

"Yes, how did you know?"

"I have been expecting you. You will understand soon. Tell me, Mr. Scott," she said, "Why are you here?"

Had I paused to think about the circumstances, I would have found the meeting strange and left in search of something else. I knew my time was short and I needed money fast. I did not have time to spend with a witch and her penniless partner, even if he was an old friend of my father. But I needed a Hail Mary and this was it.

"I'm dying," I said.

"Well, that is not helpful," she said. "We are all dying, Mr. Scott, some just have to wait longer than others. I need to know why you are here right now. What brought you to me?"

I thought about the question for a moment and responded, "Dreams."

"Dreams," she said, "that is more helpful. What did you see and hear in your dreams?"

I told her about the little girl and my great-grandfather and the others who were dead and those who were not. I told her that the little girl told me to take Pastor David with me and that he led me here.

"What does this mean?" I asked.

"I don't know," she said.

"Well, that is not helpful," I said.

"Mr. Scott," she said, "I knew you were coming and now you are here. I did not know why then and I do not know why now."

"Pastor David said you could help me."

"I understand many dreams and I understand your dreams brought you here."

"How did you know I was coming?"

"Your grandfather told me," she said, "but I thought you would be coming with him."

"You mean, Senior?" Jesse asked.

"If that is what you call him. I know him as Hugh but when he visits I see him as a young boy. I know him and several other Scotts. They are regulars of the marsh."

"All of them dead?" I asked.

"Yes," she said.

"You've seen them in your dreams too?" I asked.

"Yes, of course, and elsewhere," she said.

"Where? How?" I asked.

"Mr. Scott, spirits are everywhere. We can all feel their presence. We can see them in our dreams and feel them in our thoughts and hear them in our prayers and in our meditations and in whatever else you want to call the other realm. I just happen to be able to feel their presence more than most. Have you ever felt the presence of someone and then they suddenly appeared?"

"Yes," I said.

"It is like that," Ruby said. "Have you ever prayed and asked for something and received an answer?"

"Yes."

"It is like that," Ruby said. "Have you ever seen the future in your dreams?"

"Yes."

"It is like that," Ruby said.

"So, what do my dreams tell you?" I asked.

"Not much."

"What about the little girl?"

"I don't know her, but I know this, you should listen to her."

"I did!" I said. "She brought me here to talk to you but you can't help."

"What you want right now, I don't have. You want money," Ruby said.

"Yes," I said.

"I can help," Jesse said. "Mel, I need to show you something. Do you have a boat?"

"Yes, I have Dad's."

"Good," Jesse said. "My sailboat is moored nearby. I'll leave right now. You know where the marina is, the one near The Wreck?"

"Yes, I live nearby."

"That's what I thought. I'll meet you there as soon as you can get there."

"Where are we going? What do you want me to see?"

"You'll see. Mel, you need to trust me. This is no chance encounter."

"Ok. I'll see you there," I said, getting up and thanking them both.

"Mel, take Pastor David with you," Ruby said.

"I will."

"That's what the little girl said, right?" Ruby asked.

"Yes."

"And, Mel, I hope you visit me again."

"I will," I said. I understood.

We walked back down the old cobblestone road to my car. On the way, I felt his presence just as I had felt it before. His presence was strong and unmistakable but I did not tell Pastor David that Nero was near.

We put the boat in the water in the pitch, black night and waited in the river that ran by the marina.

"Look at that," Pastor David said.

To the east, the horizon glowed as the giant red moon rose, lighting up the marsh.

"Here comes Jesse," I said, seeing his boat sail our way.

All was quiet under the big moon. Jesse sailed past us and we followed. We rode slowly through the night, meandering through tidal creeks until we reached Jesse's island. Jesse sailed up a narrow creek and we followed until Jesse stopped at the edge of a deep hole.

"We are here. This is my island," he said. "You will see it soon."

"See what?" I asked.

"The gold," he said. "I have lived on this island for more than forty years. I brought you here because you are Hugh's son. Other than Ruby, you will be the only other human beings who have seen it since it sunk to the bottom hundreds of years ago. I found the first coin about forty years ago. I spent decades gathering the coins and bringing them here."

"How much are they worth?" I asked.

"Millions," he said, "maybe more."

We sat near the edge of the deep hole as the tide fell.

"No one else knows about the gold and I plan on keeping it that way," Jesse said.

"Why?" I asked.

"People," he said. "People would ruin this marsh if they knew about the gold. They would come by the thousands and they might find more gold. There is more out here. They would find a way to ruin this place. They would build bridges and roads and houses and resorts. They would fill the water with boats and gasoline. This marsh has remained untouched since the beginning of time and I plan on keeping it that way."

"So why are you showing me the gold?" I asked.

"Because you are Hugh's son," he said. "And I want Hugh's son to know that I will help his family when he is gone."

"Thank you."

"I will make sure they have enough, whatever that is," he said, "but nothing more. There is plenty here and I'll give them as much as they need when needed. I'm showing you this so you can go home tonight to your wife and let her know that she need not worry about where her next meal is coming from or paying doctor bills or anything else she needs. I will provide, but you cannot tell her about me or about the gold. I will make sure the money gets to her. Pastor David can help. We can melt some coins and sell the gold."

"Thank you," I said.

And I was thankful, but I was also tired and in pain. So much had happened in one day and the shock started wearing off and the reality of dying set in. I missed my family. I missed Lynn. I missed Tyler and I missed Sophia. I would have traded all the gold in the world for time but no one could give me time.

We sat together in silence on the bank of the creek under the light of the moon. I watched the water as the tide went out and I wished I were like the tide. The tide never died. There was no beginning or end. It went back and forth like a pendulum on a clock. But the tide never stopped.

I trusted Pastor David and I trusted Jesse. I trusted that there was gold somewhere on Jesse's island and that he would share it. I trusted that my family was now rich. I had found what I was looking for and I felt low and depressed. I wanted to go home.

I knew now that Lynn and Tyler and Sophia would find their way, even without the gold. We had always found our way. I knew now that I wanted, more than anything, to be with them as we found our way. I wanted my baby girl to run and give me a great big starfish hug. I wanted to watch Tyler hit another pitch and grow through all the challenges of being a child. We did not need money. We needed each other.

"I want to go home," I said. "Jesse, I trust you and I trust Pastor David. I don't need to see the gold. Your word is enough. I should go home now. I should spend time with my family."

"I understand," Jesse said, "but we cannot leave now. The tide is too low. We must wait until it begins to rise again."

We sat still and quiet in the night. I watched the tide fall lower and lower as if it were the slowest clock on Earth. I did not want to speed up time, but I would have given anything to speed up that tide. Then something ever so slight broke the silence. I heard a distant ringing in my ears and the hair on my neck rose.

"Did you hear that?" I whispered.

"No," said Jesse.

"No," said Pastor David.

Then I felt it and I knew. This was the third time I had sensed his presence. He was on the island now.

"We need to hide," I whispered.

"Hide?" Jesse said. "From what? We are already hidden. No human being lives within ten miles."

"We need to hide now," I said. "I can feel it. Someone else is here on this island."

"Ok," Jesse said. "Follow me to my house."

We stood up to follow Jesse through the woods.

"Stop right there! All of you!" a voice said.

I turned around to see Judd and Mori Nero, their pistols trained on the three of us.

"Keep your hands where I can see them!" Mori said.

My eyes met Judd's.

"Mel Scott?" Judd said. "Mel Scott. What in the hell are you doing here?"

I just stared at Judd, not saying a word.

"You know him?" Mori asked.

"Yes," Judd said. "You don't remember Mel?"

"No."

"He's just some punk kid I knew in Sandy Pines."

"That means he knows us too," Mori said, looking at me. "He'll be the first to go."

"What do you want?" Jesse asked.

"You know what I want, crazy old man," Mori said. "Where is it? Where is the gold?"

"Now, what would a crazy old man do with a bunch of gold?" Jesse said.

"Don't waste my time old man," Mori said. "You tell me where it is now or Mel is dead."

"It sounds like you want him dead anyway," Jesse said. "Go ahead and shoot him."

Mori smiled.

"You think I'm kidding around," Mori said. "You think I won't shoot this punk kid?"

"I know you will," Jesse said. "But I hold all the cards right now. After you shoot him, shoot me next. The gold dies with me."

The full moon now rose high above the five of us standing in the middle of that island, lighting up everything around us. Behind Mori and Judd, something small caught the moon and sparkled. It was a coin. As the tide went out, more appeared. I could now see the tip of an underwater mountain of gold.

Judd looked at me again.

"Mel, what are you doing here?" he asked.

"I think I know now. Look," I said, pointing to the pile of gold that grew behind them.

Mori and Judd turned around and saw it.

"Holy shit!" Mori said. "Look at that. Now who holds the cards, old man!"

They turned around, but we were gone.

CHAPTER 36

## *The Final Fight*

We followed Jesse through the moonlit maze of palms and oaks and shrubs until we reached his tall house. We ran inside and locked the door.

"Here," Jesse said, handing each of us a rifle. "The ammunition is on that shelf," he said, pointing to a small shelf on the wall. "I'll climb up top and keep a lookout. Just do what I say. We have food and water and ammunition."

The walls were thick. Jesse had built the lighthouse-structure out of tabby—true tabby, using mortar from oyster shells.

"These walls will take a bullet," Jesse said. "We need to keep them outside. Man the door!"

Jesse climbed up the steps that spiraled up along the wall.

"They're here!" Jesse said, "about thirty yards from the door. Just keep them out. We can hold up here for days."

My heart sunk. I did not have days.

"They are not going to leave until they kill us all," I said. "I know these men. They are bad men. The worst. Judd, the younger one, was mean and ruthless even as a child. No one liked him, but everyone feared him. Mori, the older one, is Judd's father. Mori is far worse. He is not just mean. He is empty. Everyone knew that Mori beat Judd on a regular basis, probably every day until Judd grew too big to hit. I'm surprised to see them together. They hate each other. They hate everyone. They will kill us all unless we kill them first. It is the only way."

"What are they doing?" Pastor David asked.

"It looks like they are gathering sticks and palm branches," Jesse said. "They are going to build a fire around us."

"Will this place burn?" Pastor David asked.

"Not the house, but they could fill it with smoke if they make it to a window. Keep them away!" Jesse said.

"Can you call someone?" I asked.

"No. Phones don't work out here. I don't keep a radio. Until now, that's how I preferred it."

"Does anyone live on any of the islands nearby?" I asked.

"No. We are alone."

I knew that something must be done. None of us had days. I put my ear to the door, trying to listen to what was happening outside.

"Dad," Judd said, "let's fill the boat up while we can and go, before the tide rises too much."

"And leave that mountain of gold! You really are a fool," Mori said.

"We could take all we need and get away before daylight."

"And leave this friend of yours here? They know our names," Mori said. "I'm not leaving until everyone else is dead, kid."

"We could fill the boat and then set this island on fire," Judd said. "No one will see it until tomorrow, and probably not then. That gives us all night to get away. We can go anywhere with that gold."

"Shut up, you idiot," Mori said. "You listen to me, you understand. I ain't leaving no gold here!"

Pastor David heard too.

He looked at me and said, "Forgive me, Mel. It is the only way."

Pastor David put down his rifle and walked out of the door.

"What are you doing!" I yelled. "Come back!"

"Look at this!" Mori said. "A god-damned blessing walking right into my lap."

"What is he doing?" Jesse asked.

"I don't know," I said. "He just walked out."

"Hands in the air, preacher!" Mori yelled.

Mori put one arm around Pastor David, shielding himself from us while putting the pistol against Pastor David's head.

"You look here!" Mori yelled. "I hold the cards now, old man. Make it easy on yourself and come join the preacher."

I leaned against the door, my mind racing. What was Pastor David thinking! We had an advantage with three men. Now we were down one and they had him. I needed to do something and I knew what it was. My training from long ago took over. Run toward gunfire. This house would be my coffin if I did not act. Run toward gunfire. That is what Pastor David did, except he left his weapon. Run toward gunfire, I thought, waiting for the right moment.

"You don't have to shoot him, Dad," Judd said. "We can take him with us."

"Shut up, you fool! And don't call me Dad!" Mori said.

"He is our ticket," Judd said. "As long as we have him, we have time. We can take him with us on the boat until we get far enough away."

"Shut up!" Mori said. "They don't think I'll shoot him and neither do you."

"Your son is right," Pastor David said. "Take me with you. You can kill me now or kill me later. I am dead either way. Take me with you and you will be safe."

"You are all fools!" Mori said. "Don't think for a second that I put any trust in a preacher's word. I learned that long ago. You will get your death wish, preacher man. Don't worry about that."

Jesse climbed down the steps.

"Give me a rifle," Jesse said.

I handed him Pastor David's rifle.

"Can you get a shot?" I asked.

"I doubt it, but what else can we do?"

"None of you think I'm serious!" Mori yelled. "That is because you are all fools. You have five seconds, old man! If I don't see your face in five seconds, then I'm bringing a dead body to your doorstep!"

Jesse ran up the steps.

"Don't shoot him!" Judd said. "You don't have to shoot him! His dead body doesn't help us."

Mori laughed.

"There ain't no us, kid. And it ain't his dead body I'm leaving, it's yours."

When the gunfire erupted, I burst out the door in a rage, expecting shots to rain down on me. Then I saw them and I stopped.

Mori's body lay on the ground. Dead. Judd knelt over him, crying. Pastor David stood beside Judd, his hand on Judd's head.

"What happened?" I asked.

Neither spoke. Judd cried while Pastor David prayed for him, but he whispered and I could not hear what he was saying.

I walked toward them.

"Stand back!" Judd said, standing up with his pistol trained on me. "Both of you. Get back! Now!"

"You don't have to do this, Judd," I said.

"Get back! I'll shoot. Just like I shot him. Get back and leave me alone!"

I stepped back and Pastor David walked over to me.

"Judd," I said. "We will go back to the house and leave you here. Take whatever gold you want. It's yours. You have my word, we'll give you time to get away from here."

Judd pointed the gun at me and then at Pastor David.

"Back up!"

"Judd, you can take me with you if you don't trust me. You can even shoot me. All I ask is that you promise not to harm my family."

"Shut up!" he said. "I don't want to hear about your family!"

"Judd, please. Take me and as much gold as you want. I will help you carry it. It's an easy decision."

"Back up!"

"Just promise you'll never harm my family."

He looked at me and shook his head.

"You still don't get it, do you?" he said. "You never did have to worry about your own family."

Then he looked at Pastor David.

"Preacher," Judd said, "no one ever cared."

Then he raised his gun and fired.

## CHAPTER 37

# *The End*

As the shot rang out, a thick fog rolled in, the kind of fog that comes out of nowhere on a clear night and covers everything around it. I walked through the fog toward Judd. Something or someone pulled me toward him. I sensed it. I felt it. I knew it even though I could not see it. Then I saw her. The fog cleared away, revealing Judd's body next to his dad's. Beside his dad's body sat a little boy. He was weeping with his hands in his face. Near him, stood the little girl I had seen before. She walked over to the little boy and touched him on the shoulder. He looked up. The little girl leaned over and hugged him. He wept while she hugged him.

"It will get better," she told him.

The little boy looked up and wiped tears from his face and I saw him. I had seen him before, at recess when he was in the first grade. I recognized every freckle.

The little girl walked over to me.

"He had never been hugged before," she said. "He needs to be alone right now. It is time for us to go."

We walked through the fog to Jesse's house. Pastor David followed, none of us saying a word. We met Jesse at the door.

"They are both dead," I said.

Jesse nodded, relieved.

"I need to go home," I said.

"Go," Jesse said. "I'll take care of all of this. Both of you, go."

The tide had risen, enough so that Pastor David and I could ease Dad's boat out of the creek.

Under the bright moon, we traveled across the marsh. I smelled the salt air and felt the cool night breeze against my face. I wondered if it would be for the last time, my last ride across the marsh.

The little girl sat next to me on the boat. She looked about the marsh and smiled, looking at everything as if for the first time. I wondered if she had ever been on a boat.

"Can you see her?" I asked Pastor David.

"See who?" he said.

"Am I awake?" I asked.

"Yes, you are very much awake," he said.

The pain in my body felt real. I looked up at the millions of stars and they seemed real. The moon seemed real. It all seemed so real yet it all seemed so far away and beyond my understanding.

"Pastor David?" I asked. "What is it all about?"

"I don't know," he said. "I don't have all the answers, but it is ok to not have all the answers. I know that now."

"But what was the point?" I asked. "My time is almost up and I still don't know the point of it all. I feel like I have spent my entire life struggling, going nowhere and ending up nowhere. What was the point?"

"Mel, every day is a struggle. It is not just ok to struggle—it is good to struggle. You struggle because you have hope. You taught me that."

"What are you saying? I have not done anything in my life. I have not accomplished anything. I am going to leave this life with nothing to show for it. Even all the gold on Jesse's island seems useless now."

"Mel, can't you see what you did for me? You never turned me away. You treated me like a human being and a friend. Through my experiences with you and your family, I found hope. Hope is a gift and you gave it to me."

I looked at him and nodded, thinking about my family and my mom and Gilbert Lyle and Pastor David's transformation.

"I was lost, Mel, so lost that I did not even struggle. I needed to struggle."

"I see," I said.

"Mel, you are struggling. There are many others who are struggling. Your family will struggle. But in their struggles, they will find strength in hope. It is the only way. And I promise that I will do my best to help them see the hope in their struggle."

"Thank you."

"Mel, it does not stop with you or me or your family. You have been a part of something that is more than we can imagine, more than we can understand. Your spirit will outlast your body. Your gift of hope will outlast your time on Earth. You have already helped spread hope. That hope will double, I promise, and it will double again and double again and again until the day when hope blankets this planet and can double no more. It is the only way. And you will have been a part of that."

"Thank you," I said. "I hope you are right."

We rode the rest of the way in silence. As we pulled the boat up to the marina, I looked once more at the stars against the night sky. I looked across the marsh toward the ocean as it all glistened under the moon.

"I can walk from here," Pastor David said. "You need to go home now."

"Thank you," I said. "Thank you for everything."

He smiled and walked away.

"Can I go with you?" the little girl said.

"Yes," I said.

We got in my car and drove home. On the way, I saw the first flake and then another and then another.

"Look at that," I said. "It never snows here. I must be dreaming."

"No, not yet," the little girl said.

The snow came down so hard I could barely see the road. By the time we pulled in my driveway, the snow stopped, leaving a white blanket across the yard.

"It is a beautiful home," the little girl said.

"Yes, it is," I said. "My family is inside that home."

We walked around back where I could see inside through our living-room windows. All the lights in the room were on. I watched as Lynn and Tyler and Sophia decorated the house. They all seemed so happy. It smelled like Christmas and I could hear music playing through the windows.

Sophia ran to Lynn and held her hands. Tyler joined them as Sophia's sweet voice sang one of her favorite songs.

"Wing-a-wound the wosies!
A pocket fuhl of posies!
Ashes! Ashes!
We all fall down!"

They fell down rolling and laughing about the living room, still unaware that I stood outside looking in.

"I am going to miss the sound of my children laughing," I said. "I will miss that sound more than anything, I think. I hope I can remember it near the end."

I looked down at the little girl beside me. Like my children, she was happy and smiling.

"You know this place, don't you?" I said.

"Yes."

"You have been here before?"

"Yes."

"You know my family?"

"Yes."

"You were in my van when we drove down here?"

"Yes."

"You were with me all along, weren't you?"

"Yes."

While looking at my family dancing about the room, I asked the little girl, "Is that heaven?"

"It was," she said.

Looking at my family, I thought about all the joy they had given me. I now realized that my time with them had been a gift, a gift I had taken for granted. I wondered if the little girl beside me had once had a family like mine. I hoped that the sight of them brought her joy.

"Do you have a name?" I asked the little girl.

"I think you were going to call me Rosa."

## A Note From The Author

*Thank you for reading this book. It was written to be read more than once. I hope you find the time again.*

*Sincerely,*

*Jeff*

*P.S. A sequel will follow. It will begin where this one ended.*

*www.acrossthemarsh.com*

Made in the USA
Columbia, SC
26 March 2020